PLAY *in the*

PRIMARY CURRICULUM

Edited by Nigel Hall and Lesley Abbott

Hodder & S

A MEMBER OF THE HODDE

British Library Cataloguing in Publication Data

Play in the primary curriculum.
  I. Hall, Nigel II. Abbott, Lesley
  372.190941

  ISBN 0 340 53805 8

First published 1991
Impression number 10 9 8 7
Year   1998 1997

Printed in Great Britain for Hodder & Stoughton Educational, a division of Hodder Headline Plc, 338 Euston Road, London NW1 3BH by Redwood Books, Trowbridge, Wiltshire

Contents

About the editors and contributors

Nigel Hall is Senior Lecturer in Educational Studies at the School of Education, Manchester Polytechnic. He is a specialist in early developmental literacy and has written numerous articles on literacy and 'play and literacy'. He is the author of *The Emergence of Literacy*, and the editor of *Writing with Reason: the Emergence of Authorship in Young Children* (both published by Hodder & Stoughton). **Lesley Abbott** is Principal Lecturer in Early Childhood Education at the School of Education, Manchester Polytechnic. She has a particular interest in the role of play in the education of young children and has organised and contributed to numerous courses and conferences on this theme. She was a member of the government Committee of Inquiry into the Quality of Educational Experiences offered to three- and four-year-old children (the Rumbold Committee).

Janet Atkin is a lecturer in Education in the School of Education at Nottingham University. She is a leading authority on the education of young children and has lectured and written extensively on this subject. **Catherine Coleman** has completed the PGCE course at Wolverhampton Polytechnic. She now teaches at an infant school in Jersey. **Helen Dutton** has completed the B.Ed course at Manchester Polytechnic. She now teaches at St. Peter's Primary School in Preston. **Susan McCaldon** is deputy head teacher at Ravensbury Primary School in Manchester. She also contributed a chapter to *Writing with Reason*. **Fiona MacLeod** is a nursery teacher at Eastwood County Primary School in Bury. The work detailed in this chapter was carried out while on an M.Ed course at Manchester Polytechnic. **Jill Paulin** was, when the work for this chapter was carried out, a teacher in Hong Kong. She is now Headteacher at St. Augustine's Primary School in Kilburn. **Laura Sparrow** is headteacher at Heald Place Primary School in Manchester. She has contributed chapters to a number of publications. **Helen Strahan** is Senior Lecturer in Education Studies at Manchester Polytechnic. The work for her chapter was carried out while the author was on secondment at Manchester Polytechnic to look at structured play in the primary school. **Steven Tyler** is an Educational Psychologist for Stockport Education Authority. He was previously Research Fellow in the Department of Psychology at the University of Keele, where he worked with Corrinne Hutt. He is the author of the Keele Pre-School Assessment Guides.

Introduction
Nigel Hall and
Lesley Abbott

Play is one of the most common features of children's everyday lives.

> *Once outside, he glanced cautiously around and slunk down the road in the direction of his home. Then he doubled suddenly and ran down a back street to put his imaginary pursuers off his track. He took a pencil from his pocket and, levelling at the empty air, fired twice. Two of his pursuers fell dead, the rest came running on with redoubled vigour. There was no time to be lost. Running for dear life, he dashed down the next street, leaving in his wake an elderly gentleman nursing his toe and cursing volubly. As he neared his gate, William again drew the pencil from his pocket and, still looking back down the road, and firing as he went, he rushed into his own gateway.*
>
> *(Crompton, 1983)*

There can be few, if any, adults who cannot recall imagining themselves as the hero or heroine in an event that was acted or dreamed with a high level of involvement and intensity. The intensity of William's re-enactment is matched by Garrison Keillor's recollections:

> *There for years, to the peak of Paradise, we resorted every day, the old gang. Nobody said, 'Let's go'; we just went. Lance was the captain. Rotting trees that lay in the clearing were our barricades, and we propped up limbs for cannons. The boulder was the command post. We sat in the weeds, decked out in commando wear – neckerchiefs and extra belts slung over our shoulders for ammo and Lance even had a canteen in a khaki cover and a satchel marked USA – and we looked down the slope to the*

roofs of the town, which sometimes were houses of despicable white settlers who had violated the Sacred Hunting Ground of the Chippewa. We sent volleys of flaming arrows down on them and burned them to the ground many times, or we pounded the boats with tons of deadly shells, some of us dying briefly in the hot sun. 'Aiiiiieeee!' we cried when it was time to die, and pitched forward, holding our throats. There were no last words. We were killed instantly.

(Keillor, 1985, p. 11)

There is an undeniable macho component to these two examples. This kind of masculine association begins early as Paley (1984) suggests when discussing the four-year-olds in her kindergarten class:

Every year, the girls begin with stories of good little families, while the boys bring us a litany of superheroes and bad guys.

This kind of imaginative play may be replaced in the minds of some young females by fantasies with 'My little pony' or more domestic events but the power and intensity, as well as the enduring memories of early play events, are significant for both sexes (see Chapter 1 in Singer and Singer, 1990).

This very commonness is probably what gives play a 'taken-for-grantedness' in the minds of most adults. Utterances such as 'Go outside and play' and 'What are you playing at now?' are heard and reheard hundreds of times by young children. However, young children learn very early that things which are intensely pleasurable usually have their less fortunate consequences. Play, being something that apparently does not have to be worked at, is deemed less valuable by society than those activities which have outcomes that are susceptible to educational evaluation.

It is no secret among educationists that we have been singularly unsuccessful in persuading politicians, journalists and parents that play is of tremendous significance in the intellectual, social and physical growth of children. So long as we are talking about very young children, the pre-fives, no one worries too much. But once children start schooling most parents consider that 'real' learning has to start and the apparently inconsequential behaviours associated with play must, fairly quickly, be replaced by 'work'.

The association between play and very young children has been reinforced by the weight of research addressed to play and learning in very early childhood. The majority of studies of play have been, and continue to be, related to investigating the play behaviours of very young children. There have been relatively fewer studies of older children's play or of the place of play in the education of children within formal schooling, although it is clear that this is beginning to change.

Perhaps part of the problem lies in the way investigators have been endeavouring to define play. There are an enormous number of definitions of play and a large amount of time has been taken up arguing the merits or defects of those definitions. While is is necessary, in many circumstances, to be precise about phenomena, there are times when it is not quite so helpful. It can lead to related notions being unexplored or neglected, and perhaps more problematic still, it can lead to interesting ideas being neglected in practice.

What do we mean by this? Well, where exactly does play stop being play and become active learning, or simulation, or drama, or imagination, or even reading? Reading – why reading? Nell (1988) has described ludic reading as 'at root a play activity, intrinsically motivated and usually paratelic, that is, engaged in for its own sake' (p. 2) and has suggested that books 'envelop us in alternative realities only because we give them explicit permission to do so'. (p. 2) These two aspects are both reminiscent of many of the often suggested defining characteristics of children's play. There have also been many suggestions that symbolic play becomes modified into imagination. Singer and Singer (1990) suggest that:

> Whether in adults it takes the form of reconstructing one's past (for memory, as most cognitive research demonstrates, is rarely simply a vivid re-experiencing of actual events), planning what to do on the job, or merely allowing onself to daydream about future vacations, sexual opportunities, or space adventures, the imagination liberates us from the tyranny of this place, these chores, these people. (p. 20)

In children it is symbolic play which is used to create this 'liberation' from the here and now, and the mechanisms which maintain boundaries between reality and play are used with considerable skill by young children (Garvey, 1977 and Wolf and Pusch, 1985).

If we become too precious about the significance of differences in definitions of play then are we in danger of neglecting possibilities which transcend the formulation of precise categories? On the other hand if we stray too far from the precision of definitions about play are we in danger of all those positive qualities being diluted or maybe even lost completely?

Most commentators on play have insisted that play should retain its critical components as it permeates more formal schooling. Indeed, the first of our two contributors have this as a feature of their chapters. However, attention also needs to be given to how play might have to change, not only as it enters more formal schooling but as it accompanies children while they are growing up. One of the major problems stemming from the majority of play studies having been carried out with younger children is that much less is known about how children themselves modify play as they grow older, as they gain experience of the world, as their education increases, and as they mature physically, socially and intellectually.

Part of what is being suggested in this book is that while some essential characteristics of play are still vital, sensitive structural and intellectual intervention from teachers, far from crippling play, can in fact open it up in ways which have the potential to be extremely rich. In all the chapters in the second section of this book teachers have had a prominent role in the creation of play setting, in structuring, in providing demonstrations, and in suggesting ways in which activities might move. At the same time the children have also been given space, time and resources to make their own uses of these interventions. The teachers, while structuring aspects of the situations (and perhaps by doing so) have endorsed play as a legitimate mode of working within the classrooms. The result in these chapters is an effective working partnership between the children as critical–reality definers, and the teachers as critical–reality definers. As a result of this partnership the children develop and use knowledge that is socially sanctioned (i.e. National Curriculum and other knowledge), while at the same time they use play to generate meanings and applications for this knowledge that make sense to them.

All of the chapters in the second section root their play activities in what is sometimes called 'socio-dramatic play'. It is also referred to frequently in England as 'structured play'. However, on the whole, we prefer the use of 'socio-dramatic' (although not all of our contributors do) as many kinds of play which are not socio-dramatic can be carefully structured.

One of the most interesting features of socio-dramatic play is that it is often situated in contexts which by their very nature are event-structured rather than curriculum-structured. In other words, if you elect to create a travel agency then you take on board all the behaviours associated with travel agencies not just those which narrowly reflect one area of the curriculum. Thus in our two chapters on travel agent play it is clear that the children engaged in behaviours which transcended curriculum boundaries but which at the same time included work from within a wide range of curriculum areas. Play in reasonably authentic settings cannot be constrained within curriculum areas because in life those settings are not constrained in curriculum areas.

Once the setting becomes more complex, the nature of the decisions and plans made by the children become more complex. As scripts for play are developed so one can see clearly the relationship between play and Freud's notion about thought, that thought is 'trial action'. That is indeed what socio-dramatic play is, but it is overt rather than internalised into purely thought. However as 'trial action' it allows exploration without too much fear of, or cost from, failure.

The chapters in this book show attempts to create reasonably authentic settings within classrooms in which children are allowed to play. That is, they can use these settings in ways that they feel are appropriate. Sometimes children use these settings to play in ways that seem to deny the existence of the settings. However, more often than not, the settings facilitate imagination, provide contexts for new forms of expression, and open up new choices for children.

In Section One we offer two chapters which give a background to some of the issues which have dominated the study of play.

In Chapter One, 'Play in relation to the national curriculum', Stephen Tyler examines play in the context of early years education and examines the implications of the Education Reform Act for the continued existence of play in the primary curriculum. He outlines an historical perspective on the relationship between play and early years education, considering ideological, psychological and educational factors. He then reflects on the position of play in the National Curriculum and the extent to which the simultaneous demand for assessment might be detrimental to the continuation of play in classrooms. He concludes that there is no necessary reason why play should be excluded from classrooms as a result of the imposition of the National Curriculum.

In the second chapter in this section 'Thinking about play', Janet Atkin examines the background of mistrust about play which exists in the minds of so many parents, politicians and even some teachers. She points out that 'play' is not only a pursuit of children, but is a natural part of the life of adults. However, adults are, for many reasons, suspicious of the sheer pleasure of play. She then explores reasons why play, despite being of demonstrated educational value (as reviewed in Stephen Tyler's chapter), does not feature as frequently in classrooms (and particularly in infant and junior classrooms) as one might imagine. She concludes by suggesting some ways in which teachers might examine their own positions on play, pleasure and work.

In Section Two of this book we offer a series of case studies in which practising classroom teachers explore a play activity which they have set up in their classroom or school. All the case studies belong to one area within play – socio-dramatic play.

In 'Down at the Chippy', Fiona MacLeod shows how the real-life setting of the local fish and chip shop was able to provide a wonderful play setting in her nursery classroom. Her three- and four-year olds were linked into a variety of encounters and experiences in setting up their 'chippy'. These were planned and structured by Fiona. However, once the 'chippy' was established it was the children's to explore in any way that they wished. The resulting play was both rich and pleasurable. The talk became more sustained and fluent, and allowed the children to explore a range of social roles, as well as other curriculum activities.

In 'Play and writing', Helen Dutton, teaching six-year-olds, set up two play settings, a hairdresser and a café. She made sure that although she did not direct the play she did provide a range of natural resources, many of which related to literacy. She observed the use the children made of these 'props' in their play and found a rich and dynamic range of writing resulted. This writing covered a range of functions and was used by the children not as an academic exercise but to facilitate the sustenance and development of the themes of their play. She suggests that although play will never offer a sufficient experience for the whole of the writing curriculum, it does offer opportunities for using writing in a range of semi-authentic contexts, and thus can contribute to writing being seen as a meaningful and purposeful activity.

In a small-scale private survey, Janet Moyle (personal communication) found that teachers very rarely associated play with historical learning. This is somewhat surprising given the development in the last ten years by many historical centres of providing opportunities for children to dress up and act out historical roles when visiting those centres. Sue McCaldon in her chapter 'In the olden days' tells how she made use of play to help very young children develop historical understanding. What is important to note is that play had a role within a wider set of experiences. The play was not forced into carrying the main burden of developing historical understanding. It existed alongside a range of different experiences which combined to create highly effective opportunities for four- and five-year-olds to gain a sense of the past. Her class, within the topic of 'change' created in the classroom an 'old house'. They also watched television programmes, made visits, and most importantly met and talked to a wonderful elderly lady who was able to provide first-hand accounts of life in the 'olden days'. Sue is able to show how the children's perceptions of past events began to change as their experiences in the classroom increased. The play had a central role in this shift in allowing children to play in a way which forced them to explore the meanings of life in the past. She says, 'It was as if playing made sense of it all.'

In 'We're all going on a summer holiday' and 'Play and knowledge of the world' Catherine Coleman and Jill Pauling, respectively, examine how geographical knowledge can grow within play settings. In Catherine's chapter, she describes in some detail how the activities were set up and grew as the children's knowledge and experience increased. She demonstrates how structuring of experiences can make play a much richer experience for children in creating diversity and depth. Some teachers who are interested in play are reluctant to actually try it because they are unsure how to go about it. Catherine's chapter gives a strong and clear outline of all the processes she and the class went through to develop an area which allowed powerful links with many other curriculum areas as well the development of aspects of geographical understanding.

Jill Pauling's chapter concentrates less on how the play was set up and more on what happened within it. The richness of the learning is conveyed powerfully by the extraordinary conversations of the children, and the delightful writing that grew out of the play. It is important to note that in both Catherine's and Jill's chapters the teachers were active in helping children to explore the setting in ways which almost forced the children to move forward in their knowledge and thinking. However, this powerful drive to move forward was never carried out in ways which prevented the children from engaging in play which was pleasurable, motivating and educational. For teachers of older infants or juniors who wonder whether play can have a role further up the school, these two chapters offer a convincing 'yes' response.

In 'The airport as one world', Laura Sparrow and the team at her school developed a play setting that was deliberately non-curricular. It arose mainly out of the school's desire to root their multicultural education in activities that demanded fundamental changes in response rather than ones which were superficial and rather trivial. By selecting their theme carefully the school was able to involve the children in play situations which demanded the sensitive evaluation of other people, and highlighted the need for cooperative enterprise, where engagement transcended race, gender and class.

Helen Strahan in her chapter 'From the station to the hotel' tackles the problem of introducing play into the junior curriculum. She worked in a school where very successful whole infant department play settings were developed. By engaging the older children in the infant's play, the older children and their teachers were persuaded that play had something to offer education in the later years. Finding play in junior schools is pretty rare, yet this chapter shows that it can be done in ways which children and teachers find beneficial.

All the chapters in this book reflect the beliefs of the authors that play has a role in schooling. There is a vitality to the children's involvement in play that is simply too precious to lose. It is also a wonderful opportunity for teachers to observe how children make sense not only of their own worlds, but how they are attaching meanings to the knowledge that they are acquiring from more formal settings. It is something of a paradox that while one of the principal aims of education is to enable children to function in the complex world that exists outside and beyond schooling, that in schooling we separate the real world into categories that seldom exist so purely outside of schooling. By being event-situated, socio-dramatic play settings allow children to explore the complex relationships that exist between people and situations.

In one sense socio-dramatic play can be conceived of as subversive in educational settings in that it challenges rigid curriculum distinctions. By trying to recreate a degree of authenticity within classrooms it challenges the curriculum to make itself relevant and appropriate to real-world conditions.

Although we are making strong claims about retaining play as an important vehicle for learning in classrooms, this stance should not be read as a claim that all learning can take place through play. We view play as one medium through which learning can be undertaken and observed. However, we hope that the chapters in this book will show that not only are play and learning mutually compatible, but that play can be fully endorsed by the aims of the National Curriculum and, indeed, in some circumstances is a more successful way of achieving them.

References

Crompton, R (1983) *Just William*. London: MacMillan.

Garvey, C (1977) *Play*. London: Fontana Books.

Keiller, G (1985) *Lake Woebegone days*. New York: Viking.

Nell, V (1988) *Lost in a book: the psychology of reading for pleasure*. Harvard: Harvard University Press.

Paley, V (1984) *Boys and girls: superheroes in the doll corner*. Chicago: University of Chicago Press.

Singer, D and **Singer, J** (1990) *The house of make-believe: play and the developing imagination*. Harvard: Harvard University Press.

Wolf, D and **Pusch, J** (1985) The origins of autonomous texts in play boundaries in GALDA, L. and PELLEGRINI, A. (eds) *Play, Language and stories*. New Jersey: Ablex Press.

1 Play in relation to the National Curriculum
Stephen Tyler

Introduction

The Education Reform Act 1988 introduced a range of innovations which presaged an era of radical change to the educational system in this country. The implementation of the Act, and in particular the introduction of the National Curriculum, has elicited a great deal of discussion in educational circles. Some educationists have expressed concern over the value of some of the reforms and the potential threat that they pose to what has been perceived as accepted 'good practice' in teaching in our schools. While some authors have raised a spectre of a curriculum strangled by tests, in the teaching of which teachers will resort to increasingly formal didactic approaches, others have focused upon the stress that such profound changes and the rapidity of their introduction may induce in the teaching force. It may be argued that this stress in itself may cause teachers to abandon some elements of practice which while of value to the education of the child in the broadest sense are not seen as central to the delivery of the curriculum. This would be especially true, perhaps, of elements of practice which are time-consuming with regard to preparation and whose value is not necessarily fully recognised outside of education. It can be argued that any change in practice may induce a degree of stress and anxiety during both the periods of anticipation and of transition itself. However, at the present time it remains to be seen whether the fears that the National Curriculum will radically alter the nature of primary schools, in which play constitutes such an important part, are to be realised.

Traditionally, play has been the activity of childhood and its educational value in the early years of education has been championed by any number of notable figures from Rousseau onwards. One of the perceived threats is that the enhanced role of assessment in the new curriculum may lead to increased formality in tuition style and a diminution of the role of play which may permeate downwards through the infant school and even into the nursery. This chapter argues that this is not a necessary consequence of the implementation of the Education Reform Act.

The nursery tradition

Before considering the National Curriculum and the consequences that it may have for education in the early years, it is perhaps worthwhile to reflect upon the historical background to the ideas that underpin the world of nursery and infant education. Although interest in the pre-school child has been particularly great over the past thirty years, the history of concern for the education and welfare of the child below the age of five extends over a far greater time-span. Prescriptions for the socialisation and tuition of the young child occur in classical writings, but formal provision for instruction outside the family is principally a phenomenon of the last two centuries.

The pioneering work in the foundation of pre-school provision occurred at the same time as a change of attitude towards children in society. As Blackstone (1971) points out, one of the apparent differences between industrial societies and other social systems is the higher level of prestige allocated to children in the former.

> A new philosophy has grown up which maintains that the needs of the child ought to be given consideration before all others. The child belongs to the most privileged age range in the advanced industrial society and demands are constantly made that its rights should be respected. Sacrifices made by adults on behalf of children do not receive scorn on the grounds of undue sentimentality, but are applauded as virtuous acts of unselfishness.
>
> (Blackstone, 1971, p. 8)

The industrial conditions of the late-eighteenth and early-nineteenth centuries focused attention on the needs of what were termed the 'infant poor'. These needs centred upon the child's health, his education and his play. Not until the early-seventeenth century had children begun to emerge as social entities in their own right, and even then the concept of childhood was limited to the first few years of life (Aries, 1973). Thus the writings of Rousseau and some of his late-eighteenth century contemporaries mark the beginnings of a radical change in attitude and approach to child rearing. Whereas earlier authors had instructed their readers to deal sternly, if not harshly, with their children, Rousseau desired his to:

> *Love childhood, indulge its sports, its pleasures, its delightful instincts. Who has not sometimes regretted that age when laughter was for ever on the lips and when the heart was for ever at peace? Why rob these innocents of the joys that pass so quickly, of that precious gift which they can never abuse? Why fill with bitterness the early days of childhood, days which will no more return for them than for you?*
>
> (Rousseau, 1762, p. 43)

These sentiments were central to subsequent attempts to found both nursery and primary education.

The history of education in the early years is well documented (Blackstone, 1971; Crowe, 1973; Van der Eyken, 1974; Bradburn, 1976; Bruce, 1987; David, 1990). Two strands in the development of the provision may be distinguished (Blackstone, 1971). The first is the concern for the health and welfare of the child and recognition of the need to protect children from exploitation by parent or employer. This concern ultimately led to the view that positive provision to care for working-class children was necessary in order to compensate for deficiencies of the home. The second strand is composed of an interest in the education of the young child and is initially identified with a small sector of the middle-class who founded institutions from the conviction that children needed additional or alternative stimulation to that provided by the home, however good the general standard of care within it. These strands, the compensatory and the strictly educational are closely intertwined in what may be termed the nursery tradition (Woodhead, 1976), and are extant, albeit in modified form, today.

At a practical level the nursery tradition emanates from the work of pioneers such as Robert Owen, Margaret and Rachel McMillan, and Susan Isaacs (Van der Eyken, 1974). In addition, early years education has drawn heavily from developing psychological and educational theory. Of perhaps greatest import here is the work of Friedrich Froebel, Maria Montessori and Rudolf Steiner (Bruce, 1987). As Bruce points out, the work of these pioneer educators with young children and their families reveals a set of common principles which have endured and which still influence much of current nursery and infant practice. Bruce identifies these principles as follows:

1   Childhood is seen as valid in itself, as a part of life and not simply as preparation for adulthood. Thus, education is seen similarly as something of the present and not just preparation and training for later.

2   The whole child is considered to be important. Health, physical and mental, is emphasised as well as the importance of feelings and thinking and spiritual aspects.

3   Learning is not compartmentalised for everything links.

4   Intrinsic motivation, resulting in child-initiated, self-directed activity is valued.

5   Self-discipline is emphasised.

6   There are specially receptive periods of learning at different stages of development.

7   What children can do (rather than what they cannot do) is the starting point of the child's education.

8   There is an inner life in the child which emerges especially under favourable conditions.

9   The people (both adults and children) with whom the child interacts are of central importance.

10   The child's education is seen as an interaction between the child and the environment, including in particular, other people and knowledge itself.

(Bruce, 1987, p. 10)

The work of more recent educationists and psychologists such as Bruner and Piaget, develop but implicitly support the principles of the early childhood tradition which can be seen in action in the majority of our nursery and infant schools today. These principles are central to what may be identified as the ideology of the pre-school world.

The ideology of early years education

A nursery (and to some degree the reception class) may be seen as a recognisable social world which is clearly differentiated from the social worlds of the home or of the primary school. It may be distinguished by the ideas held by the nursery practitioners about the nature of young children and the learning processes of early childhood. These ideas, many of which are presented above, are seldom explicitly expressed in everyday life since they are so fundamental and central to the work of the teachers who hold them as to make their expression unnecessary. Only when nursery teachers are questioned by researchers do these ideas become explicit (Hutt *et al.*, 1989). Nevertheless, although they may remain hidden for much of the time the ideas themselves are not dormant and in combination form a coherent body of thought or ideology. King (1978) describes the ideology of the infant teacher, which received official recognition in the Plowden Report. That of the nursery teacher is clearly similar although there are important differences. First, the nursery teacher places if anything an even greater emphasis on childhood innocence. Secondly, whereas the infant teacher's ideology may reveal a degree of ambivalence towards play, contrasting it with work which is of implicitly greater merit, no such ambivalence exists in the ideological framework of staff in nurseries (Hutt *et al.*, 1989). In the infant school the range of didactic methods is comparatively great, encompassing as it does both formal instruction and discovery learning. In the nursery, although a certain element of structure pertains, this tends to be covert, and the emphasis is clearly upon play as the method of knowledge and skill acquisition.

The belief in the efficacy of play in the facilitation of the child's development may be seen as a third strand of the nursery tradition. Whereas the strands outlined by Blackstone are concerned with the functions of the nursery, this last strand is methodological. Its origins are to be found in the writings of Pestalozzi and Froebel, who urged that children should be provided with the opportunity and liberty to develop their spirit through free and unfettered activities. In the statement of the case for play in early childhood, the activity became invested with almost poetic qualities:

> *Play is the purest, most spiritual activity of man at this stage, and at the same time typical of human life as a whole . . . It gives . . . joy, freedom, contentment, inner and outer rest, peace with the world. It holds the sources of all that is good.* (Froebel, 1887, p. 54)

Later authors have gone further to suggest that not only is play beneficial but also instinctive, spontaneous and essential for the normal development of the child. The currency of similar views is apparent in more modern writing on pre-school provision. Thus, Cass (1975) states:

> *Yet play experiences are vital to all children; the very essence of play is that it is an end in itself; there is no compulsion about it; it can be taken up or lain aside at will for its own final justification. Children not only discover themselves in their play, they begin to understand the behaviour of people and things.*
>
> *(Cass, 1975, p. 17)*

and McCreesh and Maher state:

> *The importance of play for all children cannot be overemphasized. For the pre-school child play is a means of coming to grips with his environment. His first discoveries of his world are made possible through play. His language and thought are developed in play situations. His social and emotional development are supported and developed through play. His physical and mental well-being are assisted through play.*
>
> *(McCreesh and Maher, 1976, p. 20)*

As suggested earlier, it may be argued that in the infant school, teachers recognise a distinction between work and play, though the differentiation between the two activities is by no means clear-cut and is largely situation dependent (King, 1978). In the nursery no such distinction is felt to be necessary. However, as the child progresses through the educational system so the tension inherent in the distinction between work and play appears to increase for our colleagues amongst the teaching profession (and for parents and administrators). Certain forms of play, such as day-dreaming, may even be seen as reprehensible. Yet there is no necessary conflict here since play and work are merely ends of a continuum, and in part the differences are semantic.

Play is an umbrella term. Its opposition to work suggests its optionality, but its principal characteristic is a lack of constraint. Thus, for example Dearden (1967) defines play as: 'a non-serious and self-contained activity which we engage in just for the satisfaction involved in it.'

In play the player has potential control of a situation which in real life he may not be able to approach. Play is fun.

Play in the early years

Numerous explanatory theories of play have been propounded which illuminate some of the observed characteristics and apparent functions of the activity (Hutt, 1979a, 1979b). In the main, the theories are complementary to each other since they emphasise different features of play (although it must also be stated that some are clearly contradictory). That this should be the case is hardly surprising since all the behaviour of children except for eating, sleeping and elimination, has in one context or another been called play. The view that such behaviour is beneficial is, therefore, difficult to oppose given the plethora of theories to which recourse may be made. As Sylva and her colleagues have commented:

> *If the child stands against the garden fence for ten minutes staring absently around him, they (teachers) claim he is learning by observing. If he repetitively puts dough into balls they say that 'the new baby at home is causing him to regress and he needs this simple act'.*
>
> *(Sylva et al., 1980, p. 48)*

Thus, for some early years practitioners all that a child does in his play may be construed as valuable to his development. Many different types of play may be identified (Jeffree *et al.*, 1977; Hutt, 1979a). Yet it is also generally recognised that superficially similar activities may have different qualities associated with them. Parry and Archer (1974) indicate that there are two levels of play, one which merely keeps children occupied, while the other contributes to their educational development. The implication is clearly that some forms of play are more beneficial to the child's development at any particular time or stage. Tyler (1984) has argued that it is possible to assess the quality of children's play in various ways and in particular with recourse to the taxonomy of play developed by Corinne Hutt (Hutt, 1979a). For the sake of the later discussion of the National Curriculum it is worthwhile reconsidering this model. Hutt's taxonomy of play has Piagetian undertones, distinguishing between epistemic and ludic aspects of play, each category being further subdivided as shown in Figure 1 (Hutt, 1979a; Hutt *et al.*, 1989). While epistemic behaviour is concerned principally with the acquisition of information, knowledge and skills, ludic behaviour involves the rehearsal of materials already acquired. The difference is similar to Piaget's distinction between accommodation and assimilation, although it permits us to go further by allowing us to categorise common activities within a theoretical framework (Tyler, 1984). Arguably, conceptual games

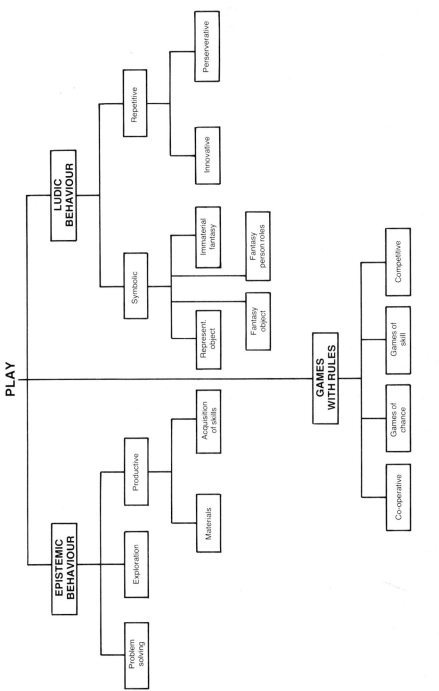

Figure 1 A taxonomy of children's play (After Hutt, 1979a)

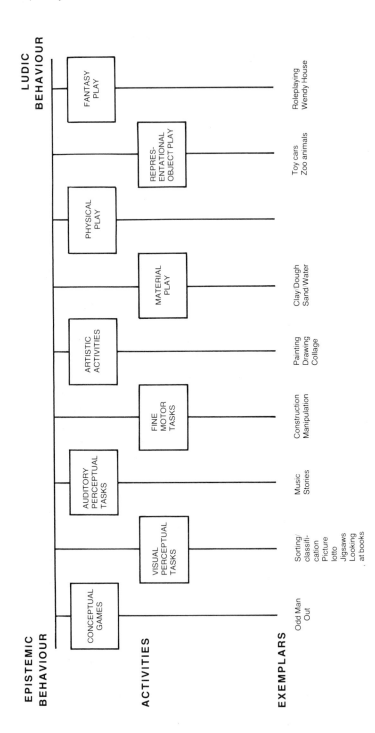

Figure 2 Classification of children's activities in the nursery (from Tyler, 1984)

and tasks requiring auditory or visual discrimination are more typically biased towards the epistemic end of the play spectrum, whereas fantasy and physical play are more usually loaded towards the ludic end (see Figure 2). On any one occasion, however, any particular activity may have greater or lesser ludic or epistemic elements. Thus, when an activity is novel it may attract epistemic behaviour, whilst upon attaining familiarity it may be incorporated within play which is essentially ludic in nature. Curtis (1986) provides an excellent example of how epistemic and then ludic behaviour patterns may follow each other in one extended play sequence. In this example, which commences with an adult-initiated challenging experience, the group of four-year-old children exchange a problem-solving situation for a fantasy one upon apparent mastery of the challenge.

> *The children were confronted with a hole in the ground about two metres wide, half a metre deep and some five metres in length. They were told by their teacher to imagine that this was a very deep river which they had to cross and which was too dangerous for them to swim. After being presented with the challenge the children began discussing the issue freely, each one entering fully into the spirit of the activity. By 'chance' the teacher had placed nearby a collection of rope, pieces of wood, tyres, etc. which might be helpful in solving the problem. During the next 45 minutes the children worked diligently seeking ways to cross the river referring to the adult where appropriate. The teacher never allowed the children to become frustrated but helped only by guiding them to make their own 'discoveries'. Eventually the children solved the problem and an appropriate bridge was constructed . . . What followed was a perfect illustration of Corinne Hutt's theory. Once the problem was solved and all the children had safely crossed to the other side of the river, the concentration, the elaborate, methodical and scientific discussion ceased and the bridge turned into a 'boat'. Some pieces of wood became oars and the children paddled down the river singing nursery rhymes as they went. The new activity gave rise to much merriment, more language, but of a very different kind, and considerable fantasy play. The boat remained the centre of imaginary play on several subsequent occasions during the ensuing weeks.*
>
> *(Curtis, 1986, p. 130)*

This example illustrates very neatly the facets of epistemic and ludic behaviour. Overall, it may be argued, there may be a balance to be struck between the two facets if the well-being of the child is to be nurtured. If a child exhibits an overwhelming preponderance of epistemic behaviour patterns, there is a danger that although learning is occurring, generalisation through the application of the skills and concepts is not. Similarly if a child spends an undue proportion of his time engaged in essentially ludic forms of behaviour, there is a genuine danger that he may be missing out on situations in which the acquisition of fresh knowledge may occur (Tyler, 1984).

The central tenet that children learn through play is supported by empirical evidence. A now classical piece of research by Sylva *et al.* (1974) described the role of play in the problem-solving activities of pre-school children. In this study it was found that children who were given opportunities to play with equipment before being required to use it to solve a problem tended to complete the task more readily than those who were not permitted to engage in play with the equipment beforehand. Other studies have refined the experiment in realisation of this finding. Learning, in the sense of acquiring information from a novel or unfamiliar source, is, however, not a necessary consequence of all play. If more ludic episodes commence before thorough exploration of the source is complete, learning in the pure sense may be prematurely curtailed (Hutt, 1970). But it cannot be doubted that play can facilitate all aspects of learning and the experience of countless teachers in early years education intuitively supports the research findings. Anybody who remains sceptical of this conclusion has only to read Michael Armstrong's account of how successful an educational experience even such an apparently simple task as making a cotton reel tank can be (Armstrong, 1980).

Much recent work has centred upon play and what has come to be termed cognitive challenge. Observations of children's play in the nursery in the research projects of the seventies and early eighties suggested that to a rather worrying extent children's play appeared to be lacking in cognitive challenge (Tizard *et al.*, 1976a, 1976b; Sylva *et al.*, 1980; Meadows, 1982; Clarke, 1988; Hutt *et al.*, 1989). However, to say that this remains the case in all nurseries in Great Britain would be both untrue and unfair. Nursery staff have listened to the researchers' suggestion that there was a need for more structure in the provision made for young children. This is not the opaque structure represented by the adoption of formal didactic styles but rather a transparent structure as viewed from the perspective of the child. Transparent structure consists of a framework of materials and discrete guidance as exemplified by the illustration of the teacher's role in the activity described by Curtis above. Whereas in the past staff may sometimes have been tempted to assume that learning is bound to occur through the provision of the appropriate materials, they are now ensuring this intellectual growth through skilful intervention and more precise monitoring. In addition, it may be argued that teachers in the early years have become increasingly aware that children in nurseries and infant schools may acquire abilities at an earlier age than was thought possible a few years ago. The work of researchers such as Margaret Donaldson and Martin Hughes is now well known and has had some considerable influence in changing attitudes. Thus, whereas until comparatively recently Piaget's notion of the pre-operational stage had emphasised the limitations of the young child, these workers have shown us that the child may be capable of much more if the conditions are right. It may be argued that early years educators who have adapted their practice in accord with the research findings of the last fifteen years, while retaining their commitment to the traditional principles reviewed above, are well prepared for the current implementation of a National Curriculum.

The National Curriculum

The Education Reform Act 1988 provided for the establishment of a National Curriculum for schools in England and Wales, comprising a core curriculum of English, Mathematics and Science and Technology, together with a prescribed list of other foundation subjects. This National Curriculum, which is seen as part of the whole curriculum, and which emphasises the child's right to studies which are both broad and balanced, is to be taught to all pupils of compulsory school age. Within the curriculum there are appropriate Attainment Targets (ATs) divided into different levels. Programmes of Study and assessment arrangements. The Act defines Attainment Targets as:

> The knowledge, skills and understanding which pupils are expected to have at the end of each key stage.

and Programmes of Study as:

> The matters, skills and processes which are required to be taught to pupils of different abilities and maturities during each key stage.

The four consecutive Key Stages are the years of compulsory schooling which end when the pupils in a class are seven, eleven, fourteen and sixteen years of age. Assessment is conducted by a combination of the teacher's own assessment, for which guidance has been given, and the results of the application of Standard Assessment Tasks (SATs) at the end of the Key Stage.

Inspection of the documentation which surrounds the National Curriculum indicates that much of the content of the curriculum in the different subject areas is already familiar to teachers, although the balance between the time allocated to different subjects and in some cases the emphasis within them may represent a change from the past. Teachers of children in the early years will be particularly interested in the first level in each Attainment Target since it is implied that the majority of five-year-olds will achieve Level 1 at the stage of the reception class. It is worth, therefore, considering a number of Attainment Targets at this level. Take, for example, Science Attainment Target 9 which concerns the development of knowledge and understanding of the structure and main features of the Earth and the atmosphere and of their changes over time. At Level 1 on this Attainment Target the pupil is required to know that there is a variety of weather conditions. The relevant part of the Programme of Study suggests that:

> *Children should collect, and find differences and similarities in, natural materials found in their locality, including rocks and soil . . . They should observe and record the changes in the weather and relate these to their everyday activities.*

This example, taken at random, seems to fit well with much nursery and infant school practice and this point appears to be general to other Attainment Targets, even if the title of the Target appears to be far removed from the tuition of young children. Let us examine another target from the subject area of Mathematics. Attainment Target 5: Number/Algebra is concerned with the recognition and use of patterns, relationships and sequences together with the ability of the child to make generalisations. At Level 1 the child should be able to:

> *Copy, continue and devise repeating patterns involving one digit numbers represented by objects/apparatus or one digit numbers.*

The examples given are:

> *Continue a threading bead pattern: red, red, blue, red, red, blue . . .*

and

Continue the pattern 21212121 etc.

Again, although we may not always recognise that we are teaching the early stages of algebra in the activities we pursue in the nursery or reception class this is indeed the case.

It is reassuring then that much of the content of that part of the National Curriculum designed for the youngest age group of children within compulsory education is consistent with the good practice in early years education in the recent past. Also, it may be contended that many of the statements contained within the publications surrounding the National Curriculum echo or are congruent with the ten principles underlying the early years tradition identified by Tina Bruce, listed earlier. Consider, for example, the third of the principles, that learning is not compartmentalised, with this statement from the working party on Science in the National Curriculum:

> *In the early primary stage, children are learning mainly through first-hand experience about their immediate surroundings. With the help of the teacher they develop important skills, concepts and attitudes. Children do not see the boundaries between one form of knowledge and another at this stage.*
>
> (DES, 1988, p. 8)

It may be argued, therefore, that the implementation of the content of the National Curriculum does not represent a particularly radical change and does not necessarily signify a threat to good practice in either the nursery, where it is not to be implemented but which may still be affected by its introduction, or in the infant school. The National Curriculum does not limit the teaching methods to be adopted and it is clear that at Level 1 (and at later levels) appropriate Programmes of Study could be taught through play-based activities.

Assessment and play

If the content of the National Curriculum in terms of the Attainment Targets and the associated Programmes of Study do not threaten play in the early years, what of the assessment procedures that are necessarily entailed?

Although Isaacs (1929) encouraged the careful observation of children, the introduction of assessment and recording in the early years is a comparatively recent phenomenon. Individual records of children's activities and progress were discouraged because of the detrimental effects of labelling (David, 1990) and this fear has again arisen recently in the discussions about assessment of children upon entry to school in the wake of the implementation of the National Curriculum. What seems to be in dispute here is not so much assessment itself, because arguably all teachers make some judgements about children and the activities in which they are engaged, but the purpose to which the results of the assessment process may be put. It has been argued elsewhere that there is much benefit to children in having their progress in different areas carefully monitored and recorded (David and Lewis, 1989; Tyler, 1989) and this has been increasingly recognisd in nurseries and reception classes in this country. Moore and Sylva (1984) discovered that more than half of the 125 local authorities that they sampled in a survey of assessment and record keeping in pre-school provision had some form of standard records. To facilitate the process of record keeping and assessment, nurseries and reception class teachers have often adopted systems of criterion-referenced testing such as the *Keele Pre-school Assessment Guide* (Tyler, 1980) or the *Manual for Assessment in Nursery Education* (Bate, Smith *et al.*, 1978). Indeed, in many instances teachers are employing their own forms of assessment which they have developed to meet the particular needs of the children in their schools. The same point may also be made of their colleagues in infant education. Although the records may be kept for different purposes (Moore and Sylva, 1984; David, 1990) there does not seem to be evidence that the consequence of adopting assessment procedures is always a move to more formal approaches. Indeed, Tyler (1980) argues that assessment procedures are often best carried out with young children by incorporating them within play settings. Anecdotal evidence would suggest that this is often done in early years education.

The National Curriculum, play and early childhood

The preceding paragraphs propose that there in no necessary incompatibility between the National Curriculum and approaches to learning which emphasise the utility of play. However, it is arguable that some threats to good practice in the early years may still have to be faced during the course of the next few years as teachers acclimatise to the changes associated with the implementation of the National Curriculum. One threat to good practice may come from those who are not in sympathy with it, who do not subscribe to the principles of the early years tradition and who seek to return to more formal and rigid tutorial techniques. To counter this threat, teachers in the early years may once again have to explain why informal techniques incorporating learning through play are valuable to children. The other two threats to current good practice are rather less obvious but perhaps more dangerous. The first stems, as outlined in the introduction to this paper, from possible reactions among staff to the process of implementing the National Curriculum. Although those most involved in the development of the National Curriculum have sought to reassure teachers that the task confronting them is manageable, it is clear that high levels of anxiety continue to be generated by teachers charged with putting the Curriculum into practice. Under the strain of what they may perceive as the many conflicting demands being made of them some teachers may yield to a temptation to adopt a more formal approach as a coping strategy. Although, as has already been noted, the National Curriculum does not specify particular teaching methods, its implementation may lead teachers to change styles through the inadvertent pressure applied. It may be argued that this eventuality may be averted by recognition and management of teacher stress, and in particular, by recourse to even greater team-work within our schools. The latter may not only lessen some elements of workload but may reinforce the shared belief in certain practices. A second effect may be to change our view of play with perhaps even greater emphasis being placed upon activities associated with epistemic behaviour and rather less upon ludic activities. On the basis of the arguments presented in an earlier part of this chapter this too would be a shame. As Alice Yardley points out, play should not be just a vehicle for other ends, it should be an end in itself (Yardley, 1984). There is still a fear that there will be a 'top-down' effect on pre-school provision, the child being subject to criteria dictated by later school requirements rather than what is perceived to be right for the child at this stage (David, 1990). What is needed again is a robust re-assertion of the principles and practices of early years education.

The last point is illustrative of the notion that children are entitled to a childhood as well as to an education. Our view of play is inextricably linked with our view of childhood, which is, as we have noted before, a comparatively recent sociological phenomenon (Aries, 1973). The notion of childhood, and with it our perception of play, may itself be under threat not from educational reform but from more general social changes (Postman, 1982). Postman argues that childhood is dependent upon education and in particular is predicated upon the skill of reading. Before the advent of the printing press and general literacy, the distinction between childhood and adulthood was much less clearly demarcated, because in an oral culture there is no way of denying children access to the secrets of the adult world. Once the child has learned to speak adequately, he has access to all forms of knowledge. By contrast the written word permits control of information. Whereas in the oral culture childhood is relatively brief and poorly defined, in the literate society it is likely to be extended and more clearly differentiated from adulthood. Postman continues by suggesting that in a televisual world, where information is once again difficult to control,the differences between children and adults are becoming blurred. Arguably, these changes in the underlying notion of childhood will ultimately affect early education much more than the National Curriculum.

References

Aries, P. (1973) *Centuries of Childhood*. Harmondsworth: Penguin Books.

Armstrong, M. (1980) *Closely Observed Children*. London: Writers and Readers.

Bate, M.; Smith, M.; Summer, R. P. and **Sexton B.** (1978) *Manual for Assessment in Nursery Education*. Windsor: National Foundation for Educational Research.

Blackstone, T. (1971) *A Fair Start: The Provision of Pre-school Education*. London: Allen Lane.

Bradburn, E. (1976) *Margaret McMillan: Framework and Expansion of Nursery Education*. Redhill: Denholm House Press.

Bruce, T. (1987) *Early Childhood Education*. London: Hodder & Stoughton.

Cass, J. (1975) Play, in *State of Play* (Ed.) London: BBC Publications.

Clarke, M.M. (1988) *Children Under Five: Educational Research and Evidence*. London: Gordon and Breach.

Crowe, B. (1973) *The Playgroup Movement*. London: Allen and Unwin.

Curtis, A.M. (1986) *A Curriculum for the Pre-school Child*. Windsor: NFER-Nelson.

David, T. and **Lewis, A.** (1989) Assessment in the Reception Class, in HARDING, L. and BEECH, J. R. (eds) *Educational Assessment in the Primary School*. Windsor: NFER

David, T. (1990) *Under Five – Under-educated?* Milton Keynes: Open University Press.

Dearden, R. F. (1967) The concept of play, in PETERS, R.S. (ed.) *The Concept of Education*. London: Routledge and Kegan Paul.

Department of Education and Science (1988) *National Curriculum: Science for Ages 5 to 16*. London: HMSO.

Froebel, F. W. A. (1887) *The Education Of Man*, (Trans. W. N. Hailmann). London: D. Appleton.

Hutt, C. (1970) Specific and diversive exploration, in REESE, H. W. and LIPSITT, L. P. (eds) *Advances in Child Development and Behaviour*. Vol. 5. New York: Academic Press.

Hutt, C. (1979a) Towards a taxonomy of play, in SUTTON-SMITH, B. (ed.) *Play and Learning*. New York: Gardner Press.

Hutt, C. (1979b) Play in the under-fives: form, development and function, in HOWELLS, J. G. (ed.) *Modern Perspectives in the Psychiatry of Infancy*, New York: Brunner Mazel.

Hutt, S.J.; Tyler, S.; Hutt, C. and **Christopherson, H.** (1989) *Play, Exploration and Learning: A Natural History of the Pre-School.* London: Routledge.

Isaacs, S. (1929) *The Nursery Years*. London: Routledge and Kegan Paul.

Jeffree, D. M.; McConkey, R. and **Hewson, S.** (1977) *Let Me Play*. London: Souvenir Press.

King, R. (1978) *All Things Bright and Beautiful?: A Sociological Study of Infants' Classrooms*. Chichester: Wiley.

McCreesh, J. and **Maher, A.** (1976) *Pre-school Education.* London: Ward Lock Educational.

Meadows, S. (1982) Assessing children's play in nursery schools, *TACTYC Journal*, **2**, 2, 25–9.

Moore, E. and **Sylva, K.** (1984) A survey of under fives record-keeping in Britain, *Educational Research*, **26**, 2, 115–20.

Parry, M. and **Archer, H.** (1974) *Pre-school education*. Schools Council Research Studies. London: Macmillan Education.

Postman, N. (1982) *The Disappearance of Childhood*. New York: Delacorte Press.

Rousseau, J. J. (1762) *Emile*.

Sylva, K.; Brunner, J. S. and **Genova, P.** (1974) The role of play in the problem solving of children 3–5 years old, in BRUNER, J.S.; JOLLY, A. and SYLVA, K. (eds) *Play: Its Role and Development*. Harmondsworth, Middlesex: Penguin.

Sylva, K., Roy, C. and **Painter, M.** (1980) *Childwatching at Playgroup and Nursery School*. London: Grant McIntyre.

Tizard, B.; Philips, J.P. and **Plewis, I.** (1976a) Staff behaviour in pre-school centres, *Journal of Child Psychology and Psychiatry*, **17**, 21–33.

Tizard, B.; Philips, J.P. and **Plewis, I.** (1976b) Play in pre-school centres – Play resources and their relation to age, sex and IQ, *Journal of Child Psychology and Psychiatry*, **17**, 251–64.

Tyler, S. (1980) *Keele Pre-school Assessment Guide*. Windsor NFER-Nelson.

Tyler, S. (1984) Carrying out assessment with young children, in FONTANA, D. (ed.) *The Education of the Young Child*. (2nd ed.). Oxford: Basil Blackwell.

Tyler, S. (1989) *Techniques of Assessment: from the past into the future*. Paper presented at the TACTYC National Conference, Worcester, May 1989.

Van Der Eyken, W. (1974) *The Pre-school Years* (3rd ed.). Harmondsworth, Middlesex: Penguin.

Woodhead, M. (1976) *Intervening in Disadvantage: A Challenge for Nursery Education*. Slough: National Foundation for Educational Research.

Yardley, A. (1984) Understanding and encouraging children's play, in FONTANA, D. (ed.) *The Education of the Young Child* (2nd ed.). Oxford: Basil Blackwell.

2 Thinking about play
Janet Atkin

Janet Moyles, in her recent book *Just Playing?* (1989), asks whether the vital issue of play in educational contexts could be relegated to the bottom of any ladder of importance, as the National Curriculum begins to dominate the thinking of early years teachers. While agreeing with her that this is a crucial question I would also suggest that to some extent 'Play under attack' could be a headline from any age! As long ago as the seventeenth century some parents were unhappy about the tendency for children to play, and argued that it only served to distract them from the real business of learning, which was undoubtedly centred on the 'book'. Writing shortly after his son's fourth birthday, the diarist Slingsby complained in 1630:

> *I find him duller to learn this year yn ye last, wch would discourage one, but yt I think ye cause to be his too much minding Play, which takes off his mind from his book; therefore they do ill yt do forment & cherish yt humour in a child, & by inventing new sports increase his desire to play, wch causeth a great aversion to their book; & their mind being at first season'd with vanity, will not easily lose ye relish of it.*

Despite the writings of many eminent educationists and decades of research on early learning, nothing seems to have changed. All teachers of young children are familiar with the constant need to justify to parents and others the idea that children's self-directed play is worthwhile, is not just pleasurable occupation and has value beyond the pre-school stage.

Why is this so? What might lie behind the general mistrust of play? Why do so many adults think play is valueless and denigrate its place in development? I think it is possible to suggest that most of the problems are because of muddled and distorted thinking about play and its meanings. For a start, we in the West are bedevilled by dual thinking and especially bipolar constructs or opposites, so that, for example, if something is good it is not bad and vice versa. How often do we automatically offer the opposite to words? If I say 'thick and . . . . .', 'saint and . . . . .', 'black and . . . . .', and so on, the hearer will fill in the missing opposite without even thinking about it. So children learn very quickly once they enter school that if it is play it cannot be work. Fein (1981) found that children between the ages of five and nine had very clear ideas about work and play. Work is compulsory, done for an adult, very often done alone, is subject to judgement and evaluation by others, and has performance criteria, usually right or wrong. Play, on the other hand, is voluntary, done for its own sake, often in company with others, and is subject to judgement only by self (I decide whether I have achieved what I wanted to from my play). Adults suggest and reinforce this dual thinking. How often have we heard them say, 'When you have finished your work, you can play' (which really means when you have done what I want, you can do what you want!).

Some other examples of dual thinking to ponder over include:

- If it's fun it can't be serious.
- If it's fantasy it can't be real.
- If it's free it can't be structured.
- If it's something children do it can't be for adults.

Indeed we might ask, Why is it our language has no 'good' word for adults who are healthily playful? They are called zany, or eccentric, nutty or crazy, or worst of all childish! In other words, in all kinds of subtle and not so subtle ways the message is given that it is not 'adult' to play. What distorted thinking! Growing up does not mean the end of enjoyment; surely one really good thing that teachers could do for children would be to demonstrate through their own play that being grown up does not mean life stops being fun, and indeed that work can be both serious and pleasurable.

Secondly, I believe some adults are afraid of the 'mess' and unpredictable nature of play: neither the player nor the content are under their control. After all, the essence of play is that it is voluntary and the child or player must have the freedom to say 'no'. (Teachers need to remember this aspect of the definition of play, for however play-like an activity is, it cannot be called play if it is compulsory.) Many people, though, often regard loss of control as the certain path to chaos – their ultimate terror. Very often adults with these fears were denied the chance to play well as children, and were encouraged to 'grow up' quickly and to 'be sensible'. Adults who were forced to grow up too soon seem to fear the exuberance of young children and are threatened by play situations, while the child's right to say 'no' is seen as being anti-authority and lacking in respect for adults. As a result, they repress the humour, fun and sense of freedom that play gives and fear these qualities in other people. Very often, in my experience, such people equate playfulness with naughtiness and are therefore deeply uneasy at the thought that play has a positive role in development as this challenges all the premises on which they have based their thinking about children.

Thirdly, some adults distrust the irrationality of some kinds of play. They dislike the element of unreality about play and its 'as if' or 'let's pretend' quality. Watching children at play with bricks, for example, they expect to see realistic constructions emerging and are disturbed if the children use the bricks as magic pebbles or aeroplanes. Often such people are heard asking children to 'play properly' with the materials, or as they envisage the correct use to be. Are these adults one-sided in their development, trusting only the left-hand brain activities of logic and rationality and evidence? Play with its emphasis on spontaneity, imagination, and intuition is often right-hand brain stuff. Surely, though, we need both aspects working in harmony for balanced development?

In addition, some adults distrust the fact that play is not directly utilitarian. Because it does not serve particular goals directly it often seems to them to be an inefficient way of learning; for example, what has making funny faces, playing peekaboo, singing nursery rhymes and engaging in sound play to do with learning to speak or read? Correcting pronunciation and learning the alphabet will teach children more efficiently and quickly, won't it? The fact that play has been shown to foster creativity, problem solving, lateral thinking, etc., is too nebulous for these people. Assessing the outcomes of play is not easy whereas the elementary tradition of teaching specific small steps in a graded and linear fashion suits a utilitarian approach.

Finally, I think the most important reason why play is devalued is that it is pleasurable! The Puritan ethic makes us feel guilty about fun and the pursuit of pleasure, and guilt often leads to feelings of discomfort or anxiety; in attempting to repress these feelings we will repress the thing that caused them as well. For adults, fun is often associated with irresponsibility, destruction, and self-indulgence (the lager lout will claim he is only having fun!). Fun is also the way we escape from things we find boring, and for many adults and children work and school are both compulsory and boring. Play and fun therefore cannot be part of school, which is serious and also a place where people earn a living, that is, work.

Does the kind of muddled thinking I have explored explain why, despite all the evidence about play being the way children learn, most research shows that play has little place in school? Is it surprising that researchers and investigators in the seventies and eighties, such as Corinne Hutt, Kathy Sylva, Neville Bennett, in both nursery and primary schools showed either that play was non-existent or undervalued or that it was fairly mundane and low-level. Indeed it is somewhat surprising that infant teachers do feel they are constantly justifying the place of play, as studies of classrooms show what a limited part it in fact has. For example, the investigation into the experiences of four-year-olds in school by Bennet and Kell (1989) found that only 6% of time was spent in play, while Tizard *et al.* (1988) estimated that top infants in the inner London schools she and her colleagues observed engaged in play for less than 2% of their time.

It may be that the teachers involved in these studies would offer some defence to this data along the lines of 'maybe the researcher hasn't been asking the right question – if play is a process and an attitude then it is not separate from the rest of the curriculum (whether defined in subjects or themes) but part of it (and cannot be listed separately).' Also, much of the research in nursery schools and classes, which questioned the quality of the play observed, was done a decade ago and many practitioners and advisors, supported by HMI (DES, 1989a), would claim that there is now much more adult involvement and richer cognitive challenge in the play situations in nursery classes.

The problem does seem to be more marked in primary and infant schools although whether the downward pressure of the National Curriculum, and more particularly assessment at age seven, will affect nurseries remains to be seen. Play matters for all pupils but I think we need to be particularly alert to the needs of four-year-olds and to remember that a large percentage (62.5%) of this age band are in the admission classes of schools, while only 14% are in nursery settings. Early childhood educators also have to be embarrassed at the findings of the HMI survey of four-year-olds in primary schools (DES, 1989b) that, 'the educational purposes of play and investigative work are not sufficiently understood and provided for' (by the teachers themselves, let alone their heads). It is worth noting though, that this somewhat contradicts Bennett and Kell's finding that teachers know the principles of early childhood education – but couldn't put them into practice, mainly because of perceived pressure from their colleagues and parents to get children reading. Shades of the seventeenth century again!

So let's now look at the educational purposes of play, the familiar question, 'Yes, but what are they learning?' and the problems inherent in trying to answer that question. I think it is as well to recognise at the outset that people who ask the question probably want a straightforward answer: 'they learn this, this and this'. They cannot handle the 'Well, it all depends' and 'the issue is complex', which is in fact the proper response. However, it is also worth sometimes turning the question on its head and saying some of the things children are *not* learning from play. They are *not* learning:

- to fail
- to seek right answers
- to accept what an adult tells them without question
- to parrot rote responses
- to stop doing something because they can't get it right, (particularly in the performance arts) or
- to become a spectator to others rather than a participant in whatever the field of interest.

So how to answer that question? We need to start by being sure what kind of learning is being talked about. Is it only cognitive learning on the grounds that that is what schools are for?

There are two replies to this. Firstly, cognition cannot be separated from affect – another example of dual thinking and the Western mind's tendency to categorise and separate. Secondly, if it is cognition as such, is it concepts, skills, knowledge, facts, or attitudes? Of all of these it is probably facts like 'two times two is four' or 'Paris is the capital of France' that are least likely to be learnt in play and usually the kind of learning people who ask the question are thinking of.

A more serious approach to the educational benefits of play comes from the many researchers who have spent years teasing out definitions and effects.

It is not easy and here are some of the problems.

- *Was what was being studied really play?* Most definitions of play include criteria such as 'voluntary', 'self-motivating', 'marked by zest or pleasure', yet experimental research is very difficult to execute if it cannot be planned in advance!
- *How short-term was the research?* It is the nature of funding, etc. that much educational research and experiment is short-term and effects looked for in a matter of weeks or months rather than years. Short-term effects are often lost after a period of time and some effects take years to emerge.
- *What was the design like?* Some experiments have been inadequately designed, for example, no control group, the same experimenter carrying out the testing as did the play treatment, a failure to control for the interaction with the adult or peers which may be the factor producing the improvement rather than the play, etc.
- *Is what is being observed play?* Observing alone cannot reveal the meaning of behaviour, as Smith (1986) so graphically describes. He found children somewhat desultorily swinging their legs on a barrel were pretending to be riding horses in the Wild West, while a girl assiduously washing a doll was doing so because it was dirty!

Given these problems of research and definition what can be said about the present state of knowledge about play and learning? Firstly, different kinds of play foster different aspects of learning, for example, exploratory (epistemic) play enhances problem-solving skills, while imaginative play contributes to verbal fluency, divergent thinking skills, and story-telling skills. Secondly, good quality play is not a necessary condition for better achievement on traditional measures of performance, that is, IQ tests and reading and maths tests, but it does foster other competencies that may be equally if not more important, for example self-esteem, task-orientation, attitudes to learning, persistence, flexibility and creativity. Thirdly, many things learnt through play can also be learnt through interaction with materials, other children, and in particular adults, in activities that would not be labelled play, such as meal times, discussions, outings, visits, directed doing and making (music, games, puzzles, baking, etc.).

In the light of this knowledge the challenge for early childhood educators is to accept that not all play necessarily leads to learning of a cognitive kind and to remember that children learn by many means – the flexible nature of human brains is so designed precisely to ensure that learning can take place whatever the particular environment. We need to remember that, as well as self-directed play, children also need instruction where an adult helps with skill mastery or information, which meets the children's intentions and search for competence and understanding. The major argument for play in school is, in my view, that it provides a context for children's learning that has the most meaning to them; it is as they are play-makers that they are also meaning-makers. A further challenge for the teacher of young children is to create a balance between self-initiated and teacher-initiated activity (or play?), and self-sought instruction and teacher-led instruction (or work?), and to blend these two into a harmonious whole rather than polar opposites. Perhaps the 'play spiral' of Janet Moyles provides an excellent model for the fluid and dynamic movement between various forms and also clues as to the nature of the role of the adult in the different modes from leaving alone, to sharing, discussing, supporting, through to assessing and reflecting on outcomes.

In my experience, teachers are enormously creative and imaginative people once they have fully internalised what it is they believe in and are trying to achieve with children. Perhaps reflecting on the part that play has had in their own development and the kind of thinking about it that they have themselves experienced over the years is one way towards such understanding.

Here are some suggestions for discussion at a staff meeting or for private reflection:

1 What was play like in your family? What kind of jokes did you like and do you still like? What was the role of humour in your family? How often did you laugh?

2 Did any adults play imaginatively with you? Who were they? What effect have they had on you?

3 Until what age were you able to sing, draw, paint, make something, or play music, without worrying whether you were doing it properly? Why was this?

4 Did you have enough playmates or were there reasons why these were few in number? What effect has this had? Did you have an imaginary friend (human or otherwise)?

5 What character in a fairy tale or legend do you most identify with? Why is this?

6   What did your parents say about play, about school, about work? What do you feel like now when you play with children? Is there any connection?

I want to close by emphasising that play is in the control of the player and that the spirit of playfulness which is the essence of play cannot be imposed or demanded. Play in school is therefore about freedom to learn and it remains to be seen whether the National Curriculum will eventually be a framework for learning in which play has an honourable part or a straight-jacket in which the surface appearance of play disguises compulsion and direction. The words of Alice Yardley (1978) still ring true for me, 'We do not set out to make a prescribed curriculum more palatable through presenting it in play form.'

If we want children to learn something specific we shall have to do more than present play opportunities of an open kind. If we want to foster and encourage the more general dispositions towards learning we shall have to have the courage to let children play and then to follow, support and extend their ideas and intentions in whatever direction they lead.

References

Bennett, N. and **Kell, J.** (1989) *A Good Start? Four-year-olds in infant schools.* Oxford: Basil Blackwell.

Department of Education and Science (1989a) *Aspects of Primary Education: The Education of Children under Five.* London: HMSO.

Department of Education and Science (1989b) *Report by HM Inspectors on a Survey of the Quality of Education for Four-year-olds in Primary Classes.* Stanmore: DES Publications Centre.

Fein, G. G. (1981) Pretend play in childhood: An integrative view, *Child Development*, **52**, 4, 1095–118.

Moyles, J. R. (1989), *Just Playing? The Role and Status of Play in Early Childhood Education.* Milton Keynes: Open University Press.

Slingsby, H. (1630) in POLLOCK, L. A. (1987) *A Lasting Relationship: Parents and Children over three centuries.* London: Fourth Estate.

Smith, P. K. (1986) *Children's Play: Research developments and practical applications.* New York: Gordon Breach.

Tizard, B.; Blatchford, P.; Burke, J.; Farquhar, C. and **Plewis, I.** (1988) *Young Children at School in the Inner City.* London: Lawrence Erlbaum Associates.

Yardley, A. (1978) Play in FONTANA, D. (ed.) *The Education of the Young Child.* London: Open Books.

3 Down at the chippy
Fiona MacLeod

Craig *Fish, chips, peas and chips.*
Sarah *Say please Craig.*
Craig *Alright, please, please, please.*
Sarah *Salt and vinegar?*

At which point Sarah starts to shovel polystyrene chips onto a tray, followed by a large piece of realistic-looking fish; she wraps the pretend meal untidily and hands it to Craig.

Like many teachers I find it difficult to stop thinking about classroom life once I have left the school premises. One evening while standing in the queue in my local fish and chip shop I suddenly thought why not have a 'play' chip shop in the classroom. At that point I wondered why the idea had never occurred to me before. Here was a local resource with which almost all the three- and four-year-olds in my nursery class had some acquaintance. I had been wanting to introduce a new socio-dramatic play area which would reflect aspects of the daily life of my children; the 'chippy' seemed a perfect example.

Within a couple of days I had shared my thoughts with the children. Their response was enthusiastic and the decision was agreed by everyone; we were going to have a fish and chip shop in our nursery.

I was aware that although most of the children knew about the existence of fish and chip shops, it was unlikely that all of them knew or that many of them had looked really closely at all the elements that made up such a situation. I decided to take all the children down to the fish and chip shop, so it was on with coats and scarves and we walked down the road. There are two groups of children in my nursery; one group comes in the morning and the other group in the afternoon. The morning group were not able to see the shop open but they were able to peer through the window and shout out what they could see. I was kept busy writing down their observations.

> **Darren** *We'll need a big silver counter.*
> **Andrew** *What about chips?*
> **Jemma** *Pies, sausages, beefburgers.*
> **Ashfaq** *Peas, curry. Something to carry the curry in.*
> **Jane** *The microwave.*
> **Allen** *Somewhere to keep the pies warm – my Dad has pies.*

The list seemed endless and I was really surprised by the quantity of information that we were able to collect. The afternoon children were more fortunate; the shop was open. We all managed to squeeze inside and as well as observing we bought a large bag of hot chips, drenched with salt and vinegar. This was shared between twenty-five children, two staff, one student and one mother.

On the following day we made large quantities of dough. From this, the children modelled fish, fishcakes, beefburgers, sausages, meat pies, meat and potato pies, cheese pies, sausage rolls, hots dogs, king ribs, muffins, and chop suey rolls – in fact, everything you would expect to find in a decent chip shop. That night I took the 'food' home and cooked it slowly until it was sufficiently hard to take the punishment to which my children would subject it. Back in school, small and large menus were prepared (using print as well as pictures), plus one large open and closed sign.

The staff were very conscious of the role of literacy in all this and wanted to help the children understand that print can convey meaning. We did not anticipate that the children would be able to read in any conventional sense but hoped that they would become aware that information was conveyed by some of the signs and that they could learn to recognise some of the signs and assign meaning to them.

Once the food was 'cooked' it was painted by the children. In order to make the fish, fishcakes and beefburgers more realistic, we first rolled them in breadcrumbs to give a rough texture. Our counter and shelves were made from Quadra (a multi-purpose building material we have also used for building everything from aeroplanes to dentists chairs).

The next day we were ready to open for business and made our first mistake. We chose three children to serve and the remaining twenty-two children, ignoring other nursery activities, all chose to queue up simultaneously, shouting out their orders. Unfortunately, the children who were supposed to be serving were oblivious to their customers and seemed content to pick up and handle the food.

It has been suggested that this kind of play is often repetitive, low-level, not necessarily social, and seldom involves adults. This is certainly true of what happened at first. The children had no interest in playing together, and the amount of social play was nil. Having seen this happening I decided to intervene. We closed the chip shop and brought all the food onto a table allowing everyone the opportunity to handle the goods. We counted, sorted and talked about colour, shape, size, and type of food. We did this until everyone's curiosity had been satisfied. No one missed their turn.

Mistake number two occurred during tidy time. The children did not know if all the food had been returned. We made two sets of number/food cards showing how many of everything there should be: each type of food was displayed on separate trays. On the reverse of each card were pictures instead of numbers. Because it was near the end of the school year, most of our children could count and recognise numbers up to ten. Those who could not had to ask for help, which was usually given by the other children.

We hoped that the provision of these cards would help raise the level of play for those children who had difficulty with numbers and counting. When these children joined in the play of those who could count and use the cards efficiently, those children would act as demonstrators, and knowledge would be shared. This was not observed in detail, so no further information can be given. However, there were no accounts of quarrels about counting the food, and the children managed to keep the shop organised.

The high level of interest on the part of all the children meant that for a few days the staff had to choose the children who would serve in the shop and decide when a change was necessary. There was no limit on the number of children who could queue up to be served.

On day three we allowed the children to organise themselves, and as usual they made a better job of it than we did. They decided when it was time to open and close the shop (using the sign) and decided when it was time to let someone else serve (obviously we kept a check on fairness).

We left a tape-recorder running to monitor the language and we were surprised at how much 'richer' the conversation was when the adults were not around. By 'richness' of language use I mean that there was a greater flow of interaction; the talking seemed more fluent and they were able to sustain longer, more meaningful conversations whilst taking on their roles in the chip shop. I am not suggesting that adults are unnecessary in helping children use language but sometimes in classrooms the presence of teachers can have an inhibiting effect or change, in significant ways, the types of language behaviour that occur.

Michael *Close the shop, no more food!*
Lucy *Can we have two beefburgers and chips?*
Michael *No we're closed.*
Lucy *No you're not, your sign is open.*
Michael *There's no food, just chips.*
Lucy *We want those two beefburgers there (she says pointing).*
Michael *Oh OK, then we're closed.*
Lucy *Thanks Mr Fish-man. We want chips with them.*

Marcus *Hurry up, I'm on my way to Manchester.*
Fiona *Don't nag – want a fork? Big or small peas?*
Marcus *No peas, fish and chips love.*
Fiona *Salt and Vinegar?*
Marcus *Yes, lots and lots, loads – leave 'em open.*
Fiona *Five pounds please.*
Marcus *Gosh they're cheap today! See ya.*
Fiona *Bye love.*

When adults were present, the children tended to let the adults direct the level and content of conversation; the adults did most of the talking and the children chose to respond to the adults rather than to each other. A greater degree of imagination and role-embeddedness was evident when the children were talking amongst themselves.

We wanted the children to realise how much we valued their play in the chip shop without changing their chosen direction. One way that we achieved this was to become involved from the outside of their play situation; we asked children to go on errands for us to the shop, giving instructions of the meals we would like.

> **Teacher** *Kamela, are you busy?*
> **Kamela** *No.*
> **Teacher** *Could you call in at the chippy for me and buy fish, chips and peas, with a can of coke please?*
> **Kamela** *OK, I'll write it down – I'll need money.*

Some children chose to 'scribble write' their orders on pieces of scrap paper before setting off (see Example 1).

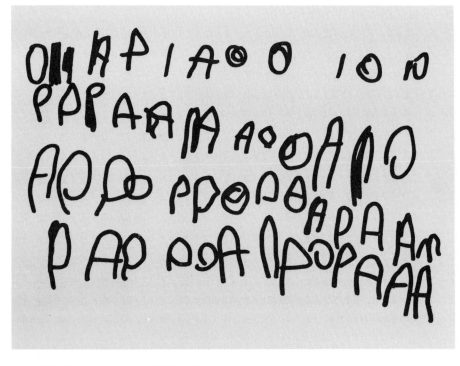

Example 1 An example of a child's chip shop order

> *Fishcake and chips, beefburger and chips, and two forks.*

We kept observational schedules of the number of children who used the chip shop over a six-week period; naturally it was more appealing to some than to others but during this time all the children used the shop in the same way. Our 'errand-sending' was a useful way of involving those children who may not have used the play situation if left to their own free choice. None of the children refused to go to the shop for us – rather they saw it as a way of helping the busy teacher who did not have a lot of time. Many children imitated our idea by sending friends with orders.

I feel that our chippy was a success for a number of reasons:

1   I had wanted it to be meaningful and within the children's experience. I feel this was successful. The environment which we created was definitely within the children's experience and did therefore, provide a positive stimulus for language growth.
2   I had wanted to promote talking and listening skills and to allow children opportunities to follow simple instructions. I feel that we made a provision for this to occur, and there was evidence that we were successful in encouraging a rich range of talk and associated listening. I feel that the 'props' stimulated language use, in particular dialogue between the children in which they really did listen to each other.
3   I had wanted to provide some mathematical experience. There was ample evidence of children sorting and matching by colour, size, and shape, and counting and handling money (although not all at the same level of understanding).

The National Curriculum is not mandatory for nursery schools. Nevertheless, it is interesting to note that the play activity I have been describing does fit in very comfortably with some of the early Attainment Targets in English. For 'Speaking and Listening' (Level One) the National Curriculum says: 'Pupils should be encouraged to speak freely, and listen, one-to-one to a peer group member,' and 'Respond to simple instructions given by a teacher'. For 'Writing' (Level one) the National Curriculum says: 'Pupils should be able to use illustrations, symbols or isolated letters, words or phrases to communicate.' And for 'Reading' (Level One) it states: 'Pupils should be able to demonstrate awareness of language in the environment (names, labels etc.)' and that: 'Pupils should be able to recognise that print conveys meaning.'

Inevitably the children in my class are only just beginning to achieve the understandings mentioned in the National Curriculum quotations. However, they are being offered a contextualised situation where those

of weeks I observed, and participated in, children's play in three different structured areas.

The first of these was a 'Hairdresser's salon'. Within days the classroom was well provided with hairdryers (including a professional 'stand-up' model), old rollers, brushes and combs, empty shampoo and non-aerosol hairspray containers and magazines, to be used by 'clients' who were awaiting the hairdresser's attention. The children gave me their ideas about what our Hairdresser's salon should look like and what equipment it should contain. As there were so many different ideas about aspects such as decor, number of mirrors and chairs, I decided that it would be best for us to vote about these matters. In this manner the children decided that the salon should be called 'Highlights', and that it should have red wallpaper, three mirrors, and four chairs. All the children appeared to be satisfied with this outcome, with those who had voted for other alternatives immediately accepting the decisions as fair.

The children were very keen to have their 'turn' in the salon and, when they did, used the telephone, appointment's book, appointment slips, and advertisement-type 'booklets' provided. I then started to examine more closely the connections between the focus of the play situation and the writing that the children produced either in or out of the play area. I kept examples of different forms of writing, especially from a mixed-ability sample of children, that I felt had been directly or indirectly influenced by the play, and it is this group's behaviour on which I shall be reporting in this chapter.

After three weeks I began to see rather static role-play situations. That is, the children were assuming the same roles (hairdresser, customers, etc.) and performing similar, almost ritualised actions. I therefore changed the focus of the structured play area, in line with the topic at that time, into an opticians, using the same methods as described for setting up the hairdressers. The children showed a fresh interest and excitement in this new situation and appeared to incorporate writing, and other literate acts, into their play more regularly. Later, a third situation, a restaurant, was set up.

I chose to set up a restaurant since, in my view, some previously present forms of writing would remain (e.g. making bookings) whilst opportunities for new forms could be introduced (e.g. menus). I would then be able to see how forms the children had used before were continued and developed and

would be able to observe if the new setting allowed for new forms
to emerge.

All the children in the class used the play area but, of course, each group
used it at a different time. Each group was able to use the area about three
times a week for about an hour each time. I used various methods to record
what was going on when the children were playing. I kept most of the
writing they produced, tape-recorded and transcribed their speech, and
made detailed and exact notes of their actions, relationships and attitudes to
one another, in and out of role. I also joined in their play when asked to or
was included by them and, sometimes, presented myself as a character in
their play, un-asked for but appropriate.

The forms of writing produced by the children appeared to be indirectly as
well as directly influenced by the focus of, and time they had spent in, the
three structured play areas. By 'directly influenced' I mean that such writing
occurred in the play area, as part of the role-play, and by 'indirectly
influenced' that either the physical presence of the areas prompted some
children to write or that role-play experiences resulted in motivation to write
and a better understanding of material about which to write.

I found that almost all the children's writing could be sorted into six
categories: letters, messages; personal notes; instructions; factual
descriptions; and stories. I will examine each of these categories.

Letters

This appeared to be the most popular form of writing, and was produced
most frequently by the class as a whole. I did not ask the children to write
letters but, as the hairdresser's and optician's were so popular, the children
obviously felt a sure way to 'get in first' with a request for a turn was to leave
me a letter or note. Such letters appeared thick and fast on the classroom
notice board every morning and afternoon and contained varying levels of
formality.

Example 1 Michelle's letter

> *Dear Miss Peplow*
> *Please can I go in the hairdresser today because I am very good at being a*
> *hairdresser because I am very good at dyeing the hair.*
> *Love from Michelle*

Michelle has fulfilled all the appropriate criteria for a letter. She begins and ends conventionally in non-speech vocabulary observing a suitable level of formality – 'Dear Miss Peplow' (to a teacher) – 'Love from Michelle' (here 'love' is appropriate to a pupil–teacher relationship). Although not spaced in three sections, the organisation of the text demonstrates that she understands the use of the salutation and closure. Michelle makes a request; tells me 'when', and gives me two good reasons why. Interestingly one of these reasons refers to specific activities Michelle plans to be involved in within the structured play area. The second 'because' statement is really an elaboration of the first.

During the children's first visit to the 'restaurant' I made the following notes:

> *Christopher was the cook. Ruth said, 'Do you want a burnt cake? The*

stupid man put them in again!' David sat at the typewriter and wrote with a crayon on headed notepaper. Ruth wrote a letter of dismissal to Christopher and pretended to strangle him. Christopher appealed, but Ruth told him it was only a warning. Ruth came to me every two to three minutes to complain that various items of food have been ruined by Christopher.

As this was the children's first visit to the 'Restaurant' they had begun by negotiating which role each of them would take. Everyone wanted to be the cook, but at this point Christopher was doing the cooking. Ruth in particular was very anxious to be the cook and was trying to make a point of Christopher's incompetence so that she could take over. As their 'parts' had been negotiated 'out of role' the only way that Ruth could make her take over legitimate was as part of the 'script'. She therefore involved the other children by asking the initial question 'Do you want a burnt cake?' and even explained why the cakes were burnt – it was undoubtedly Christopher's fault as he had put them into the oven 'again'.

In the letter Ruth wrote she assigned the name 'Robin' to Christopher, making the threat within the letter a definite part of the script, so that it could not be taken personally by Christopher.

Example 2 Ruth's letter to Christopher

> *To Robin*
> *You might have to be sacked*
> *Ruth*

Ruth had used the most powerful means of communicating her message, and this use of 'the letter' is quite different from the way letters were used during the children's play in the first two role-play situations when they tended to be written outside of the play as a means of entering the play. Indeed, the major shift across the three play settings was that when the children moved into the third setting, the restaurant, the forms of writing, and in particular letters, became embedded within the play as part of the script. A look at a couple of examples will show how this embeddedness occurred.

> **Emma** *They're eating all the biscuits. (Points to Christopher and David – both 'cooks'.)*
> **Christopher** *No I haven't. A burglar took them. (To customers – Ruth and Emma) You'll have to go now, we're closing.*
> *(Ruth and Emma complain to me about the cooks.)*
> **Me** *What do you think we should do?*
> **Emma** *Give them a warning.*
> **Ruth** *And tell them they're lazy cooks and keep eating everything.*

For the next few minutes the script of the play became the production of the following letters.

Example 3 Emma's letter

> *Dear All*
> *The cooks. We are giving you a last warning.*
> *Lots of love*

As Emma said, she wanted to 'give them a warning'. Her letter begins and ends conventionally, although 'lots of love' is not strictly appropriate here. David responded to the letter and his reply was tacked on to the end of Emma's letter:

Example 4 David's letter

Yes we are sorry to eat it.

Example 5 Ruth's letter

Dear Cook
I want you to share the food properly and don't eat all the food up at once
like a greedy animal. I would like you to be very nice to the people in the
restaurant and if you do not you will get to be sacked and you don't want
that to happen, do you?
Love Ruth

Ruth's letter was more substantial and is made particularly powerful by the condition at the end 'if you do not . . .' and the threatening question 'you don't want that to happen, do you?'

Another situation which led to letter writing occurred after a particular dramatic piece of play.

Christopher *There's a fire.*
Michelle *(to David) Manager, there's a fire.*
Emma *Pretend you can't see me, I'm trapped.*
Christopher *Pretend I'm the Fire Brigade.*
Michelle *It's a baby. It's trapped.*

A very convincing scene followed, the fire was put out and Emma and Ruth were taken to hospital. Minutes later . . .

Christopher *Pretend I smell gas and it's coming nearer and nearer.*

Christopher found the *correct* page in the telephone directory for the Gas Board, telephoned a 'repair man', and he and Michelle composed the following complaint:

Example 6 The letter of complaint

> *I am making a complaint because there is a gas leak. I thought you had mended it. Please come.*
> *The cook*

In the sequence of events leading up to the writing of this letter we can see one of the ways in which socio-dramatic play provides opportunities for the production of written forms. After Christopher has mentioned the fire, the children step 'out of role' – indicated by the word 'Pretend' – to build this idea into the script of play. Later, as if seeking a reason for the fire, Christopher mentions smelling gas. The children then attempt to construct a realistic situation as they use the telephone and write the letter, and such an important reason for them to write like this would only arise as the result of events which they could negotiate within a structured play situation.

Messages

The children were motivated by their role-play experiences and wished to contribute to the physical environment of the hairdresser's salon. They produced friezes which clearly contained a number of different messages which were presented appropriately. These appeared to be aimed at a specific audience, that is people who were 'non-hairdressers' and they were presented in the style of advertisements for the hairdressing profession. Often the form was similar to a comic strip in that parts of speech were often placed within 'bubbles'. Similiar signs and messages occurred in the other two play settings.

Personal notes

This kind of writing was produced by the children in role within the structured play areas. Sometimes it appeared as writing meant to be read only by them.

Example 7 A reminder

Two o'clock appointment for Franco

And sometimes as marks intended to be writing which could only be read (if 'reading' was an appropriate response) by them. Like real personal notes these were usually elliptical and frequently unreadable except by the person who had written them.

Example 8 Pretend writing

Such notes were sometimes made under pressure. The following personal note (Example 9) was made by Christopher, who was quickly jotting down the names of Emma and Ruth.

Christopher *Hello. Yes. What's your name?*
Emma *Emma. (Christopher writes it down.)*
Christopher *What's your second name?*
Emma *Squigglywink. (Emma walks off.)*
Christopher *Hang on! What's your little girl's second name?*
Emma *(Shouts) Squigglywinks! (Emma giggles and Christopher looks harassed.)*

Emma's booking for 10 o'clock is clearly present in Christopher's note.

Example 9 Christopher's note

While observing this situation, I noticed that when Emma saw Christopher write down her name she selected the most difficult second name she could think of and said it with satisfaction and a mischievous grin. It was a challenge to Christopher. To me, Christopher's attempt to note this name seems to be a very appropriate one, as he has made squiggles which actually look like 'Squigglywink'. I would suggest that here Christopher was not scribbling but adopting a more graphic form.

Customers noted down the times of their appointments; hairdressers and opticians wrote down appointments that were made over the telephone and occasionally ticked off a name as a new customer arrived. This form of writing, at its most extensive, tended to be 'telegraphic' and to lack syntactic links.

Another important part of maintaining the realistic situation of the restaurant was the writing down of 'orders', by the waiter or waitress. These orders (personal notes for waiters and waitresses) appeared in the form of lists of either conventional or non-conventional writing.

Instructions

The children had not been taught how to write instructions in school, apart from a small group who had recently written instructions for making a sink. However, many of the children wished to contribute to the physical environment of the structured play area and instructions were a simple way of producing a group plan and of recording, for my benefit at least, the materials they wished me to provide.

Story writing

I set various pieces of creative writing for the whole class and believe that in many instances the role-play experiences contributed significantly to the committed way in which they were written as well as to the understanding of the subject embedded in the writing.

Thursday 13th October

by Ruth

The magic Shanpoo

I went to the hairdressers and I thought he was nice So I went in and I said can I have some Shanpoo and he said no and iI said why and he said it was magic and I Said no its not and he said it was So I took it home and it was magic and I was different So I never ever went to that hairdressers agjin and that was the end of the hairdressers

Example 10 Ruth's story

The magic shampoo
I went to the hairdressers and I thought he was nice so I went in and I
said can I have some shampoo and he said no and I said why and he said it
was magic and I said no its not and he said it was so I took it home and it
was magic and I was different so I never ever went to that hairdresers
again and that was the end of the hairdressers.

the magic Shampoo
the hairdressers do
your hair shampoo
and och it day A woman
came in the
haildressers and she
sed can I have Some
magic shampoo
only If you Keep
It to you self he said
and she went
home: and she tayd
the magic Shampoo
and she said
It IS tuhnilig me
hice to kohg
and that IS the
ehd.

Example 11 Sameena

The magic shampoo
The hairdressers do your hair shampoo and one day a woman came in and
she said can I have some magic shampoo only if you keep it to yourself he

said and she went home and she tried the magic shampoo and she said it is turning me nice (?) and that is the end.

Conclusion

General conclusions drawn from my observations have clearly got to remain tentative. However, I do feel they show that children begin to differentiate between purposes and forms of written language at a very early age, and that the move into these forms derives less from instruction and more from the notion of a situation which makes contextualised demands upon the 'player' in that situation. Development appeared to have occurred simultaneously with the childrens attitude to and use of the structured play areas.

When I examined my records I was able to see that in my mixed-ability group the most frequently used form was the letter, but that considerable changes had taken place in the children's use of written forms. When playing in the hairdressers and opticians, the only form they had used was personal notes, whereas in the restaurant they used appropriately eight forms of writing as integral parts of their play scripts.

Clear changes were apparent in the letter writing. As the play developed so letters came to be used for a much wider set of purposes. That is, from being solely a means of requesting permission, to being used for sackings, resignations, invitations, complaints, confirmations, and so on. Similar developments occurred with other forms.

The significance of my children's involvement in role-play upon their production of different written forms did seem to alter noticeably as they experienced more structured play situations. It was only when they had become familiar with performing the actions and story-lines appropriate to the situations, and after experimentation with the potentialities of role-play, that they used different forms as suitable, necessary, and appropriate parts of 'the script'. Indeed, it appears that it was the development of the script of play by the children, over a number of 'visits' to a particular structured play area, which resulted in wider and extended writing. As the children negotiated roles and story-lines and put these into action, a variety of written expressions were called for and used.

These findings support my view that teachers should change the focus of structured play areas regularly to provide fresh stimuli for the use of different written forms. The involvement of the children in decision making about, and equipping of, the play areas can result in increased motivation and opportunities for purpose-specific writing to occur.

The National Curriculum English documentation has made play a legitimate classroom activity at Key Stage One. Clearly, although it is play, it also has a sense of reality about it that enables a wide range of written forms to be tackled in a purposeful and satisfying way. In the Programmes of Study for Key Stage One it is specified that children should 'Write in different contexts and for a variety of purposes and audiences'; that they should 'Undertake a range of chronological writing including some at least of diaries, stories, letters'; and that they should 'Undertake a range of non-chronological writing which includes . . . some at least of lists, captions, labels, invitations greetings cards, notices, posters'.

Play will not represent a sufficient experience for any of these but it can make a substantial contribution. No doubt all those things could be taught as exercises but I doubt whether they would be so enjoyable, so meaningful and so successful as when they can also occur within purposeful socio-dramatic play areas.

5 In the olden days
Sue McCaldon

The following account is of how 'the past' was introduced to a reception class in an inner city school. The class consisted of twenty-seven children aged between four and five years of age, who came from different social and ethnic backgrounds. The teaching of history to young children is problematic; it involves difficult and abstract concepts and has a specialised language. Some historical words have different everyday meanings which can lead to confusion in the minds of children. From previous experiences I had concluded that the role of play was significant in developing young children's understanding of the past. Play areas of an old-fashioned house and shop had given children opportunities of making sense of what otherwise could have been abstract and meaningless.

History was one element in a cross-curricular topic on 'change'. An investigation of life in great grandma's day was to be firmly based in a play area of an old-fashioned home. It was here that the children would be able to explore strange artefacts in a non-threatening atmosphere and where they would be able to see and compare differences between home life in the past and home life today.

We started the topic by viewing a *Watch* television programme about life in the past. This focused on the home, comparing a house today with one in the past. The class were quite interested in this programme but it was clear from the resulting discussion that their knowledge and understanding of the past was very limited. The children were enthusiastic about creating an old-fashioned house but not too sure about what should go in it. Although the children understood that there had been no electricity in the house in the *Watch* programme, they were not sure which modern appliances were operated by electricity. Stuart thought that we could have a microwave oven provided it was scratched to make it 'old'. From his comment it was clear that Stuart's understanding of 'old' was that it was something 'not new'.

The whole class then became involved in the creation of the old-fashioned house. We removed from the existing home corner the washing-machine, cooker, sink and television set. An old-fashioned kitchen range was created from cardboard boxes painted black. Real coal placed on red tissue paper helped towards creating a realistic effect. Artefacts were placed in the area in appropriate places; a toasting fork near the fire, a long-handled black enamel saucepan on the coals, a flat iron waiting to be heated by the fire. James was insistent that we had a grandfather clock and this was made from cardboard boxes. A rag rug was placed on the hearth, a candle in a holder on the mantelpiece, a stone hot water bottle by the bed. Now the home corner was ready for use.

The children enjoyed using the old-fashioned house. They dressed up, girls in pinafores and mop-caps, the boys in waistcoats, collars and flat caps. The cooking was done on the fire, the ironing on a table. Old newspapers were available for reading and an ancient address stamp imprinted an address on paper for letter writing. From the children's point of view the old-fashioned house could be used in much the same way as a normal home corner. There was still a table to be set, albeit with real plates, cups, saucers and cutlery, rather than the usual brightly coloured plastic variety. So it was the play involving washing and cleaning that highlighted some of the real differences.

On fine days the tin bath, washing board, dolly peg and mangle were set up in the yard, on wet days the washing was done in the corridor. Here the children cut flakes of soap from a block, dissolved them in the water, rubbed the clothes against the washing board, pounded the clothes with the dolly peg before finally squeezing the water out with the mangle. It was hard work! Some old donkey stones were discovered in the school cellar so the children gained first-hand experience of donkey stoning the steps. The rag rug was taken out of the house and beaten with a carpet beater. It was through using these artefacts that the children were able to correct misconceptions. Some children had tried beating the rag rug whilst it was still on the floor, this they discovered did not work well. From their first-hand experiences the children had a clear understanding of how the artefacts were used, unlike one six-year-old's conception of how a dolly peg was used. He had seen it displayed and had been told it was for washing and had a highly imaginative vision of how it should be used: 'You stand on it and the washing goes over the handles.' One imagines something like a washing pogo stick!

At the beginning of the topic we visited some older people living in the vicinity. Mrs B was eighty-four, slightly deaf and lived just opposite the school. Before the visit the whole class had been involved in a discussion about the questions we were going to ask. Six children went to interview Mrs B, and at this interview it was interesting to note how the children asked questions, but displayed little interest in the answers.

> **Katie** *What was the bathroom like?*
> **Mrs B** *We had no bathroom.*
> **James** *Did you have a grandfather clock?*
> **Mrs B** *(Still answering the first question) No we had no bathroom.*
> **Carl** *Did you have a great great grandfather?*
> **Mrs B** *We used to have a wash in the kitchen, in a big tub.*
> **Susie** *I think those two want to ask you something.*
> **Carl** *Did you have a great great grandfather when you were a little girl?*

Mrs B had continued answering the first question throughout the dialogue. The children seemed oblivious to her replies, their attention being focused on the questions which they were asking. Other questions asked at this interview focused on aspects which the children were familar with in their everyday lives:

- What was your front garden like?
- Did you have any trees?
- Did you have any dogs or kittens?
- Did you have any windows in your house?
- Do you have any ornaments?

These were all valuable questions for the children to ask because it allowed them to explore the similarities in the past as well as the differences. Other questions reflected their classroom experiences:

- How did you light the fire?

- How did you wash your clothes?
- Did you used to make bread?

One question, 'Were there any trains?' drew an unexpected response from Mrs B. She had misheard the question thinking it had been 'Were there any chains?', and after puzzling over this she replied: 'No we hadn't, someone had to come and empty the toilet.' There was no immediate comment from the children about this surprising piece of information, but four-year-old Dale, who had played no verbal part in the proceedings, later showed that he had indeed listened and taken this in.

The children returned to school and reported back to the rest of the class with the help of a video recording. At this stage the class were more interested in viewing their friends on TV than listening to Mrs B's reminiscences. Perhaps it was not the best medium to have chosen!

Another visit with different children produced similar responses. Mr M talked about his childhood in Pakistan. He recalled how his mother did her washing at the river using a block of soap and a wooden stick to beat the washing. The children in this group were all, bar one, Punjabi speaking. Mr M began by conversing in Punjabi but as the interview continued he switched to English. The children seemed to be content to listen, allowing the bilingual instructor to ask the questions. After some encouragement some children asked questions.

> **Emma** *Were there any cars?*
> **Mr M** *Donkeys, we rode on donkeys, no cars but some buses.*
> **Alveena** *Were there any trains?*

Subsequent discussions revealed that the children could recall little of what Mr M had talked about. They did not appear to readily identify with aspects outside of their own experiences.

In the classroom the children continued to engage in activities which reflected aspects of the past. Examples of old copy books gave them a chance to experiment with joined-up writing. An old blackboard and easel were found in the stock cupboard and dusted off for use. The class enjoyed writing on the blackboard, some practised writing their names, others experimented with joined-up writing and writing the alphabet. We attempted to make a rag rug, sorting materials and designing patterns. Information books about life in the 1900s became popular reading material, with the children vying with each other to take them home as reading books.

As the children's interest grew I started to tell the class about Maud. Maud was a friend, born in 1914, who had a fund of interesting stories about her past. Some of these I knew almost as well as Maud did! I showed the class a photo of Maud as a little girl. I told them how when she was born the family were so poor that they did not even have a loaf of bread in the house. The children were fascinated and began to ask questions:

- What about food? Didn't they have any food?
- What not even any sweets?

James could not understand what the problem was, his suggestion was to go to the local TSB bank and get some of the money they give away!

I continued to tell stories about Maud, her life at school, her friends, and how her cat had stolen some custards from the local bakers, resulting in the local policeman calling round. I wove into these stories the conditions of the times, no central heating, no electricity or running water, and how Maud's shoes often had holes in them.

Towards the end of the topic we decided to have a day at school 'in the past'. We all dressed up and tables were arranged in rows facing the blackboard. Old-fashioned lessons were to take place. I informed the class that Maud was coming in to meet them and this caused great excitement. I wondered if the children would expect to see a little girl. Alveena seemed as if she might when she asked 'Is that girl Maud coming in?' As English is not Alveena's first language it may have been a confusion with language. Carl and James quite clearly understood that there had been a passage of time and that Maud would be much older now.

On the day, Mrs B also came in to visit. The children showed her around the classroom, proudly displaying the old-fashioned house, the washing area, history books and the partly made rag rug. Then the big moment came, Maud arrived. The children gathered round. Maud enjoys talking about the past and here she had plenty of willing listeners. For more than half-an-hour the class were engrossed by what she had to say. As well as listening they asked questions, particularly about stories I had told:

James *When you were in the house did you have anything to eat?*
Emma *Did you have ten people in the house? Did you have three rooms?*

Maud confirmed that this information was correct and went on to explain how ten people managed to sleep in a house with only three rooms. She was interrupted in her explanation of what is meant by sleeping 'top-to-tail' by one child's contribution: 'One at the end and one at that end, one there and one at the bottom.'

There was a clear difference with the children's responses on this occasion to those at earlier interviews. The children were now very much a part of the conversation. They listened to the replies to their questions and asked more questions as a result. Their own experiences and growing understanding of the past were reflected in the questions they asked and the comments made.

> **Alveena** *Did you have a bath?*
> **Maud** *We had a tin bath, a long tin bath . . .*
> **Lauren** *Yeh we've got it out there!*
> **Maud** *Yes? Right, we had to carry all the water from the fountain . . .*
> **Scott** *Yeh, you had a dolly peg to wash it.*

A further question caused Maud to explain about the toilet arrangements and this evoked a response from four-year-old Dale:

> **Maud** *We didn't have an inside toilet.*
> **Tom** *What did you do if you wanted a wee?*
> **Maud** *Our toilet was in the backyard . . .*
> **Dale** *The man used to come out . . . come in your house and empty your toilet.*

Lauren asked about Maud's school experiences.

> **Lauren** *Did you know that when you went to school did the teacher walk around with a big stick and every time you talked . . .*
> **Maud** *Certainly, certainly . . .*
> **Lauren** *. . . he whacked you on the head . . .*
> **Maud** *Well, the teacher used to come round, well the headmaster mainly used to come round and bend his cane.*
> **Scott** *Yeh and he had a . . . used a big stick, a cane . . .*
> **Maud** *He used to bend it like this to frighten us and then he'd walk round the back. We had desks and we sat two in a desk, and he'd walk round the back . . .*
> **Scott** *. . . and when he was walking down the back he used to hit people on the back to get out of the way.*
> **Maud** *He used to bang the back of the desks . . . but if you were naughty and disobeyed you were called to the front of the class and you got a smack across the hand with the cane which hurt very much.*

Tom *Did you hold your hand?*

Scott *We've got a stick over there.*

Maud *He used to say 'Put your hand out' . . . and whack one huge smack on your hand.*

Katie *Did it hurt?*

Maud *It did hurt . . .*

Katie *Did you cry?*

Maud *Yes I did.*

Lauren *Didn't you know you're not allowed to talk?*

Maud *Well we knew but we still talked just like you do things you're not allowed to do.*

This dialogue reflects the children's total involvement. They had obviously listened to my account of Maud's school experiences. Scott was able to make a link between Maud's past experiences and the play experiences in the classroom. Lauren and Katie were empathising with Maud's school days, showing their concern about when she was caned. During the time that Maud talked with the class it was clear that the majority of these four- and five-year-old children were listening to, asking, and actively responding to, questions.

Further evidence of the children's interest in Maud's past and of the knowledge they had gained was reflected in their stories of long ago. I acted as scribe and punctuator for five-year-old Emma. In her story, Maud was cast as the central character. It can be seen that Emma had used elements from the stories I had told in class, information gained from the interview with Maud and her own experiences to create her story of 'long ago'!

> *One day in 1990 a girl called Maud was in bed. Here mother was making breakfast. Her sister shouted 'Get up Maud!' Maud snuggled in the bed and she counted to 3. '1, 2, 3.' Before you could count to 10 she was out of bed. She had her breakfast and then she went to school. It was her first day at school. She didn't know there was no talking. She talked to her friend. The teacher came round with his cane and he whacked Maud on her hands. Then it was dinner time. Maud went home for her dinner. After dinner she came back for her lessons. She learnt the alphabet, she done her times tables and then it was story time. The story was Snow White. She had never heard that one. She liked it. After the story it was home time. She went out of the classroom and ran to her mum. Then it was teatime. After her tea she went to bed. She got her candle and a stone hot water bottle and her great big teddy and went to sleep.*

Carl, who was just five, decided to write his own story. He wrote for a
sustained period of time, oblivious to the 'lessons' going on around him.

Example 1 Carl's story

The story he wrote covered five sides of A4 paper; he worked independently using mainly invented spellings.

> *One day Maud's sister came up to Maud and said 'Maud it's time to get up out of bed.' Maud counted '1, 2, 3', and she jumped out of bed and before you could count to 10 she was dressed. Her mum shouted 'Maud didn't you know it was snowing?' So Maud put her shoes on her feet but Maud just remembered to tell her mum that she had got a hole in her shoe. But her mum had to tell her she couldn't go out. Her mum said 'You can't go out anyway because it's dinner time.' So Maud went to the table and she ate her dinner all up.*

Writing this story involved Carl in considerable effort. However, he had set to willingly and continued, with interest, for a very long time.

It is clear from the children's responses and their resulting work that they had gained a great deal from this history topic. It had included a variety of approaches: oral history, looking at photographs, a visit to Wigan Pier, examining history books and watching television programmes. Although these undoubtedly played their part in contributing to the topics' success, I feel that it was the play involvement which had the greatest influence on the children's understanding.

It was in the play situation that they were able to use historical items, explore their uses, demonstrate their understandings, refine their understandings in the light of other children's knowledge, and generally operate in a way which integrated much of the growing knowledge about the past. It is as if playing made sense of it all. They could work out the meanings of the past more easily in their play than they could by considering things in isolation. It was in play that it all came together.

Some months after the topic had finished I worked with a group of children to make an information book about the 'Olden days'. I intended this as an assessment activity. Through talking to the children about the photographs which they themselves had taken I was able to ascertain that they could recall the topic in some detail.

Although the topic had been history-based it became apparent that many other areas of the curriculum had also been covered, particularly the speaking and listening aspects of the English National Curriculum. This opportunity to explore history through play proved to be a valuable experience to all of the children in the class and demonstrated clearly that play has a vital functional role in the development of learning, and consequently within the National Curriculum.

6

We're all going on a summer holiday

Catherine Coleman

Background

I was involved in teaching a class of twenty-one mixed-ability top infant children and, along with the other two classes in the year group, I covered the topics of 'Travel and Transport' and 'Holidays'. These topics permeated the whole curriculum, though I worked within a subject-based timetable, with set lessons of between forty-five and sixty minutes. To place the subsequent play situation into context, I will start by outlining, briefly, some examples of what the children were covering in the other curriculum areas.

Amongst other subjects in language lessons, children wrote about how they travelled to school, holidays they had been on, and their creative writing topics had included 'If I Could Fly' and 'If I Was Stranded on a Desert Island'. One boy had recently left the class to live abroad with his parents, and so the children sent him some postcards they had made. Maths lessons started by looking at multiplication (for example, the number of wings on one . . . two . . . three . . . planes, wheels on tricycles, and legs on camels etc). I later created a 'Topic Maths Book' for each child, which told the story of a family going on holiday. After reading the story, the children did the related maths (for example, telling the time at the start of the journey, counting and weighing pieces of luggage at the airport, buying perfume at the duty free shop, and getting change etc.).

The classroom I worked in was fairly small and with limited available space, the children had previously had few opportunities for structured play. Once a week, on a Friday afternoon, during 'free choice', they could play in the shop or the home corner. I nevertheless believed that the children's learning could be enhanced by developing the structured play. I appreciated that this might prove a difficult task as the children were unused to structured play, and being top infants in their final term, they may have been unreceptive to the idea.

Despite these possible drawbacks, and bearing in mind the term's topics, I thought that a travel agents would have the potential to develop learning in an exciting way and would be ideal for forging strong cross-curricular links – involving all areas at the same time. Hopefully the resulting 'whole' would be greater than the sum of its parts.

I intended the travel agents to be an ongoing project, and one which would involve the children heavily in its planning, organisation and day-to-day running. I felt that it was vital that the children saw the agency as their own, and something they themselves were 'in charge' of.

Preparation

I viewed my main role as provider of resources for the travel agents, though it would be up to the children to decide how these would be used (if at all). I started by collecting holiday brochures from high street agencies, aiming to get as wide a range as possible, in terms of destinations, accommodation, methods of travel, and (if appropriate) age groups. National Tourist Boards were also very helpful when I wrote to them requesting information. They sent many colourful posters which proved useful stimuli at the outset when the children had not yet started the travel agents. I placed the posters and the brochures around the classroom, and many opportunities for language development arose as, for example, a mountain scene in Austria was compared to a beach scene in Greece. As a follow-up activity, the children were keen to find the countries on the class globe, and map of the world. The posters were changed regularly and 'finding the country' became almost a daily competition with the children.

Starting points

We began by discussing, as a class, where people go when they want to book a holiday. Perhaps not surprisingly, the majority of the class were familiar with the words 'travel agents'. Most had been inside one and so had a good idea of what went on there. When I explained that we were going to make our own travel agents in the classroom, this was met by great enthusiasm. The children were full of ideas firstly regarding the name of the travel agents. Various suggestions were offered, including 'Lunn Poly'! Social skills were developed as the children decided democratically, by a show of hands, to use the name 'Class One's Holiday Shop'.

Next, the children thought about where people might want to go on holiday. Again, they were eager to suggest places, the majority of these being where they themselves had been on holiday. Perhaps it is an indication of present living standards that places like Majorca, Greece, America and Egypt, far outweighed Blackpool or Great Yarmouth! The globe and world map were again useful here for locating countries.

Having made a list of destinations (I acted as scribe, both for quickness, and also to avoid stopping the children's flow of ideas), the next stage was to discuss the types of accommodation people could stay in. Opportunities for language development came from the children themselves, as at first they suggested 'hotel', 'caravan', 'tent', and later on the more unusual 'cottage', 'villa', and 'apartment'.

The background of the travel and transport topic was useful when the children decided how people might travel to their destinations. 'Plane', 'train', 'car', 'ferry' and 'ship' were all suggested, as well as 'camel'! When both 'coach' and 'bus' were offered, one child said that they were the same. This led on to a discussion of the differences in buses and coaches, and it was agreed to include both, because 'coaches can go to different places'.

Finally, the children thought about the types of people that might use their holiday shop. Suggestions included: 'families', 'Mums and Dads by themselves', 'old people', and finally 'us'! It was decided, then, that anyone (who had enough money!) might want to book a holiday.

Making the travel agents

In terms of positioning the travel agents in the classroom, as I have noted, there was limited space available. We decided that the best that could be done was to move two cupboards and a table, to make a semi-enclosed area. Despite this, the children were able to become totally involved in discussing the sort of things to be found in a travel agents, and in creating the 'visual effects'. Possibly, as I had already introduced brochures and posters into the classroom, these were the first suggestions made by the children. Children chose whether to work individually, or in groups, to produce posters. Most worked in pairs and so developed not only creative and artistic skills, but also social and collaborative skills. They worked on large sheets of paper and decided on a holiday destination or a method of travel. They were also extending their ability to write in a variety of styles, for different audiences, as they used language as an aid to 'advertising'. Children regularly reported back to the rest of the class what they were doing, and the posters were displayed behind the table and chairs, along with the ones from the high street agencies.

Children worked individually to produce holiday brochures. A class discussion had determined what brochures were for and what they looked like, or what they should look like. It was agreed that they should be bright and colourful and show people having a 'nice time'. When I asked why this was necessary, the children said that if the brochures weren't nice to look at, then people wouldn't want to go on holiday, and the people in the travel agents wouldn't make any money (an indication, perhaps that even seven-year-olds have a rudimentary understanding of marketing and economics!). Most children made brochures of places they had visited on holiday, and I found it interesting to note the detail on some of them. Tom's brochure (see Example 1) prompted a class discussion with a historical perspective, as he had drawn pyramids on the cover of his 'Egypt' brochure.

Example 1 Tom's brochure cover

History was one area I had not even considered when planning the travel agents! Emma's brochure of France (see Example 2) perhaps supports the belief of some, that children are never too young to learn a second language!

this is a howteL in France and French peeple said bonJur madum

Example 2 A page from Emma's brochure

The brochures were filed in cardboard boxes on the table and cupboard tops for customers to look at.

The children decided that the next thing that was needed was a computer. This proved a popular idea and two groups of children worked hard on constructing computer terminals and keyboards using cardboard boxes. Again, attention to detail was obvious, as the children copied the order of the letters on the keyboard from the class computer, and a plug and wire were made using paper, card and glue. Simon demonstrated considerable problem-solving skills as he devised an ingenious way of running a roll of paper down the front of the 'VDU screen', so things could be written on it, as though on a computer printout.

Moving on, the children cut out colour-coded (according to method of travel) tickets, and wrote destinations on them. Thus, written language was developed, and vocabulary included: 'full fare', 'half fare', 'return' and 'single'. As well as tickets for travelling in planes, ferries, buses, coaches and ships, some children made 'car tickets'. We then discussed whether people would need a ticket if they were travelling in their own car, and concluded that these tickets would be used if customers were taking their own car on a ferry. As the task of making tickets was getting (understandably) a little repetitive, because a large number were required, I made some using a spirit duplicator. These had spaces for the children to fill in, for example, the date, the cost, and the number of passengers (see Example 3).

Example 3 A typical ticket

Adam suggested that the holiday shop needed a sign, and so the children made one. This was displayed above the posters, and the children then made flags to stick around the posters. Using a large atlas as a reference, children reproduced a number of flags each. As well as drawing on artistic talents, mathematical concepts of shapes (for example, 'diagonal line', 'triangle', 'circle' and 'star') were also required. Again, children expanded their geographical knowledge as they located (with my help) the countries on the map and globe.

As most of the holiday destinations the children had chosen were abroad,

I decided to introduce the idea of passports to the class. Using mine as an example, we discussed why passports are needed, and what sort of information they contain. When making pages for the children's own passports, I encountered the usual problem of matching authenticity and accuracy within the children's capabilities. I therefore adapted the format of the original passport to include spaces for 'name', 'age', 'address', 'place of birth', 'height', 'weight', 'occupation', 'photograph' (a head and shoulders drawing of themselves), 'countries visited' and 'official stamp'. The children used maths in a real context as they measured and weighed themselves. Observational skills were developed as they drew a 'passport photograph' of themselves, and further vocabulary related to the topics was developed. I had thought that in the space for 'official stamp' of countries visited, the children might decide to draw a pattern, or make up their own 'stamp'. Oliver, however, took the idea a stage further when he suggested: 'Like we could do a kangaroo for Australia?' This led on to another discussion, when the class considered what parts of the world certain objects or people came from. I was surprised at the extent of some of the children's general knowledge as the discussion turned into a game, where I named a person or object, and the children matched it with a country. Later on, I had access to an ink pad and a set of stamps of animals and transport pictures. The children had great (if messy and inky!) fun in stamping everything from passports to brochures and message pads. It was at this stage that the children started to become more involved in role-play, as they filled in the 'age' and 'occupation' section, and became footballers, nurses and teachers (!).

Using the travel agents

I had originally thought that the children would role-play in the travel agents at set times during the day. Initially, this would be during 'free choice' on a Friday afternoon (due to timetable constraints during the rest of the week). Everyone in the class was extremely keen to join in, and so children took turns, six at a time, to go in the holiday shop. I restricted the numbers – two children working in the agency and four customers – as space was limited. The workers in the holiday shop showed prospective customers the brochures. Customers decided where they wanted to go, how long for, how many people were going, how they were going to get there, and the type of accommodation they required. The children behind the desk worked out the cost, and gave the customer the relevant tickets. Tickets were paid for using the play money from the sweet shop.

Quite often, I found that the children were much keener to be behind the desk in the holiday shop, rather than being a customer. I had previously noted that it was the same when the children played in the sweet shop – being the shopkeeper was much better than being a customer! As a result I had to keep a list of what activities the children had done, to ensure 'fairness'.

Later on, I decided to allow them to use the holiday shop activity throughout the day, and so at any one time there would always be a group of children in the area. In so doing, I found two main advantages. Firstly, I was able to mix ability groups. Children had been used to working in ability groups for most lessons, and so perhaps did not know other members of the class as well as those in their group. Mixing up the children also meant that the slower children were helped by the more able ones in terms of, for example, reading tickets and brochures. Secondly, I was able to reinforce the learning taking place in other curriculum areas. For example, one of the day's activities might be to write a story about going on an aeroplane. The children would be learning all the relevant vocabulary: 'hostess', 'pilot', 'boarding pass' etc., but in rather an abstract context. Their knowledge and understanding of the situation was greatly enhanced if they could role-play the scene in the holiday shop. It was the children themselves who had thought of extending the travel agents in this way. They converted the reading area into a plane one day (using trollies from the home corner to serve food to travellers), and a ferry the next. With the introduction of passports, other children were needed as 'customs officials'. Hostesses were also needed to collect and check boarding passes. The children in the class were well aware of sexual stereotyping, but I was able to discourage this by suggesting that Kerry could perhaps be the pilot, and Graham might like to collect the boarding passes.

Maintaining interest

Although initial enthusiasm for the project was high, I wanted to avoid the age-old problem of the novelty wearing off and wanted to develop interest in being a customer. To do these things, I regularly introduced new items into the Agency.

Previously, I had left it to the children to make up prices for travel and accommodation as they went along. I had been concentrating on language development and did not want to introduce too much maths in the first stages. Later on, though, I made some price lists for the various destinations, ways of travelling and types of accommodation. These were displayed on a board behind the desk. I attempted to make these prices as easy to add up as possible, and so consequently a lot of the prices were rather unrealistic. I did, however, attempt to get the relationships right – air travel was more expensive than going on a ferry, hotels were more expensive than camping etc. I think that the children realised the prices were not too realistic, as during the project I had to fly to Jersey and Emma said (with a grin) 'You could go from our holiday shop – it's cheaper!' Even with simple prices per person, per night, when the cost of travel was added on, some of the sums became quite complex. Calculators were useful here.

The children had been paying for their holidays with the play money from the sweet shop. As some holidays were rather expensive, we discussed how else people might pay. All the children recognised a cheque book, and I explained, in simple terms, how it worked. The children listened with interest, and the discussion developed as Sohbia asked what would happen if someone 'forged your name'. I then explained, briefly, the principle of a cheque guarantee card. I photocopied some cheques (after blanking out my name and account number) and the customers enjoyed filling in the cheques. In return, they were given a receipt, made out by the children working in the holiday shop.

Originally, the children had 'booked' their holidays verbally. Later I introduced booking forms for either customers, or employees in the holiday shop, to complete. Thus further written language was developed as the children filled in where they were going, how they were getting there and where they were going to stay etc. I also introduced a telephone message pad for use with the play phone in the classroom.

Conclusion

As this was the first time I had introduced structured play into a classroom,

I was initially a little apprehensive. Though, theoretically, I understood and appreciated the importance of play, I was still a little unsure about the practicalities of a classroom situation. I even admit to wondering whether the children would really learn anything were I to introduce play! But I hope I have shown that the children I worked with did learn a great deal from their holiday shop. They realised that there are a variety of ways of travelling, different types of holiday, accommodation and destinations. As they created the visual effects for the travel agents, they displayed creative and artistic talents, as well as demonstrating social and collaborative skills when working together. The children were also able to use some planning and problem-solving skills as, for example, they constructed the computers.

In terms of curriculum areas, the children were able to use their mathematical knowledge in context, and for a real purpose, as they worked out the cost of their holidays, and paid for them. Some children had brought in foreign coins and notes, and so we discussed (if in a slightly simplistic way) the idea of exchange rates, as, to the children, 1000 lira seemed a small fortune! A great deal of language use occurred. Children learned new words, such as 'arrival', 'departure', 'accommodation' and 'destination' etc. In terms of written language, tickets needed to be filled in, telephone messages recorded, and booking forms completed etc.

At the time of carrying out this play project I was only able to match work with Attainment Targets in the English National Curriculum document but as other documents or committee reports have appeared it is clear that the activity begins to satisfy National Curriculum concerns in maths, geography and craft, design and technology.

In addition to my own initial doubts regarding play, I was also a little wary of how the children would take to the idea. They were unused to structured play, and I did not know how they would react to its introduction at this stage (they were in the final term of top infants, and looking forward to moving up to the juniors). But I was extremely pleased with their responses, and they were full of ideas at every stage. The holiday shop soon became one of the most popular activities. A lot of the ideas came directly from the children – like the making of the computers, the kangaroo stamps, and extending the travel agents into the reading area and including planes and ferries. I had also thought that it might be difficult for the children to work with an 'intangible service' (a holiday), rather than a 'tangible good' (sweets), but this proved not to be a real problem, and the children were quite content with buying tickets for their holidays.

A lot of the success of the project was due to the children's enthusiasm. I was lucky in that most children had visited a travel agents, and all of them had been on holiday. For play to be successful, I think it is important that it be within a real context, and something to which the children can relate. I would hope that anyone who is slightly apprehensive about the value of play (as I was) would now be more willing to suggest a theme to the children, provide a few resources, and leave the rest (within reason!) to them.

7 Play and knowledge of the world

Jill Pauling

Two of the second year infant classes were doing a project on the GPO and had set up a colourful and lively post office and parcel sorting centre in the shared area between their classrooms. A lot of careful planning and thought had obviously been put into setting up and resourcing this activity and the children had discussed the various roles and jobs of the employees. Uniforms had been provided and groups of children played in the post office all day. Parcels and letters were addressed and sent either by sea mail or by airmail and the relative times it would take to deliver were discussed. Maps and atlases were studied and letters were sent to a school in England, providing a real audience for communications.

I listened to their conversations and observed the quality of their play. It soon became apparent that the children had learned from their teachers about the workings of a postal system. What was more interesting was that a greal deal of other information was being shared as well. There were conversations about the countries of origin and the destinations of the letters and the parcels. Children were writing to grandparents all over the world and discussing the relative price of stamps and delivery time. Some children tried addressing their parcels in the script of their motherland and the wealth of literate activities that resulted from this project set me thinking.

Our school is truly international although the language of instruction is English. We have primary children from more than thirty different countries. They are very cosmopolitan in outlook and many of them were born outside Hong Kong. Their parents are mostly professional and the children may be seen to be privileged in that they come from a similar socio-economic background. On the other hand, many of them have parents who are always travelling and they are deprived of any extended family support group. The children are all ex-patriot and visit their mother countries frequently. For them, travel is the norm and they have grown up in a society where restaurants, hotels, and travel are part of their early experience. I began to wonder what geographical concepts these children might already have assimilated from their own first-hand experiences. I suspected that some of these children had already begun to build up a fund of knowledge about the world around them which would include cultural and ethnic differences as well as geographical concepts.

There are many travel agents in Hong Kong and the children would be famiiar with the idea of booking holidays and travel. I invited a group of five- and six-year-old second-year infants to create their own travel agency in school. Space is very limited so we utilised a staircase and landing leading to the roof. They were thrilled to have another play area and they first discussed all the resources they thought they would need. They asked the school caretaker for an old carpet, tables and chairs. They visited the resources centre and, with the help of the librarian, hunted for travel posters and world maps. They visited a real travel agent in Central District and observed customers coming in and out and listened to the type of information they were seeking. They collected holiday and travel brochures, and airline tickets from many countries and they set up their own travel agency at school. The name caused some heated debate but the final two choices were 'Bright Travel Agency' and 'Boomerang Travel Agency'. William came up with the winning argument – 'Boomerangs,' he said, 'always come back.' So a group of new children from the second-year infants began to play in the new area. They had some jackets and dressing-up outfits to wear, but these were rarely used.

The children seemed quite keen to establish some ground rules for their play. Erica, whose mother is Japanese and father Danish, decided that she would write a notice to go up on a wall. She wrote:

> *When you go to a travel agency you have to ask the travel agent questions. What are you going to do? Maybe I will want to go to Bangkok. You might ask whether it is hot or cold. You might ask if they have a Queen there.*

Vikram (aged six) comes from India. He wrote up a list of questions that the clients might think of asking the travel agent:

Vikram

when you go to a travel agentsi wich is the best Place to visit what is the wether. What sort of hotels What sort of instruments are there what food is ther . What Sort of clothes do they were.

how they go about. What money do they use . are ther eny robbers. do they use guns. do they use hifes.

Example 1 Vikram's list of questions

When you go to a travel agent which is the best place to visit? What is the weather? What sort of hotels? What sort of instruments are there? What food is there? What sort of clothes do they wear? How do they go about? What money do they use? Are there any robbers? Do they use guns? Do they use knives?

William (aged six) who is Malay/Italian, added these to Vikram's list:

Example 2 William's additions to the list

Name of the country?
Name of the town?
Weather?
What sort of money they use?
What language do they speak?
What sort of clothes do they wear?
Musical instruments?
What language do they speak?
Famous places to visit?

Some of these questions clearly demonstrate an understanding of cultural as well as geographical issues, although there is clearly some confusion at this age about what a tourist might want to know and those questions that could be asked more generally about a country. Several children wanted to know what the word 'continent' meant as it came up in discussions about the countries that they might visit. It occurred to me that a number of words that were being used might be unfamiliar to some of the children so I asked if they would try to come up with some definitions. I gave them no clues and no help and we made a game of it so that just for once there was no collaboration.

Laura (aged six) came up with the following writing:

Laura

gerofgy is lrnaing abot
maps and the World
a mop tells you were
places are

a controy is a place
were there is flowers

a Con tent is a
grop of Contrys
Stick togother

a time table is a sum
a travel agecy is when
you want to find abot
your holiday

Example 3 Laura's definitions

> *Geography is learning about maps and the world.*
> *A map tells you where places are.*
> *A country is a place where there are flowers.*
> *A continent is a group of countries stuck together.*
> *A timetable is a sum.*
> *A travel agency is when you want to find out about your holiday.*

Laura demonstrates the complexity of the English language. To her, a day in the country is her first thought when asked to define the word 'country', although she gives an accurate description of a continent. Similarly, she has confused a timetable with 'times tables' and says this is a sum. This is particularly interesting because at that time she had not come across times tables in school.

Silvana (aged six) offered these thoughts:

> *A continent is like Asia and Artica.*
> *A time table is clock that tells the time.*
> *A travel agency is when you want to ask questions what where is.*

This discussion of words was very exciting as it became obvious that these children had a very good idea of the world they lived in. They discussed topographical features as well as climatic differences and flora and fauna.

They took it in turns to be the travel agent and client. After taking both roles myself I sat and listened and observed. I was fascinated to find that the children seemed to be taking the formula that had evolved in discussion and were applying it to their own countries based on their first-hand experience.

I managed to tape one particular role-play situation and the transcript reveals that the children really have entered into their roles. The children involved are Daniel (aged six), Thomas (aged five), Joey (aged six), Vikram (aged six), and Lauren (aged six). Daniel starts by introducing himself and saying that he is going to tell the rest of the group, who are clients, about a trip to Phuket in Thailand. This is a popular resort that a number of people from Hong Kong visit. This play is based very much on first-hand experience.

> **Thomas** *What's the name of the town you go to?*
> **Daniel** *I think the town is called Phuket.*
> **Thomas** *What sort of money do they use?*

Daniel *I think its called dollars or notes . . . Bahts.*

Joey *What's the weather like?*

Daniel *It's really hot sometimes and sometimes it rains a bit.*

Lauren *What language do they speak?*

Daniel *Some English . . . some Japan and some Phuket.*

Thomas *What sort of food do they eat?*

Daniel *Chinese . . . seafood and there's chips and some other things.*

Lauren *How do they get round the country?*

Daniel *Um . . . they walk or some people borrow motor bikes.*

Lauren *Is there any famous places they could go?*

Daniel *Um . . . not really . . . they sometimes just go to restaurants and things like that.*

Vikram *What sort of clothes should they wear?*

Daniel *Ties of course . . . T shirts . . . garden clothes.*

Joey *I thought the men wore sarongs . . . they're something like skirts.*

Lauren *Is there many beaches there?*

Daniel *Only one in front of the hotels . . . but there's a swimming pool.*

Vikram *What sort of hotels do they have?*

Daniel *Lots of different kinds like the Mandarin hotel and things . . . that's where I stayed.*

Thomas *Do they have poor hotels?*

Daniel *Um . . . yes.*

Thomas *Like where?*

Daniel *Well there's . . . well you come out of these little huts and there's a big pool and you have to walk and there's a beach if you go down this small hill.*

Vikram *How much do you have to pay a night?*

Daniel *Well . . . nothing . . . sometimes $200.*

Later on that morning roles were reversed and Vikram was trying to sell his holiday resort. He is telling the group about Bangkok.

Thomas *Which place do you like visiting best in Bangkok?*

Vikram *The Siam Intercontinental.*

Joey *Is it fun there?*

Vikram *Yes . . . yes . . . it's fun . . . it is a very big hotel and it's got two swimming pools and the lobby is very nice . . . it's made out of marble and it's got two restaurants.*

Thomas *What continent is it in?*

Vikram *In Asia.*
Lauren *What country is it in?*
Vikram *Thailand.*
Thomas *How many hours is there in the day and night?*
Vikram *About twelve.*
Joey *What language do they speak?*
Vikram *Thai language.*
Daniel *Have you ever been on one of the Klongs?*
Vikram *Yes.*
Lauren *Is it very nice?*
Vikram *No . . . it's very dirty.*
Joey *What's a Klong?*
Vikram *It's a river.*
Lauren *How do the people live?*
Vikram *I don't know . . . some people live in houses and some people live in hotels.*
Daniel *Do they eat seafood?*
Vikram *Yes.*
Thomas *Are there any houses on stilts?*
Vikram *Yes.*
Thomas *Why?*
Vikram *Some are there but I don't know why they are on stilts.*
Daniel *What colour eyes do they have?*
Vikram *They only have blue colours and yellow colour.*
Thomas *Would it be a good place for a holiday?*
Vikram *Yes it is a good place.*
Joey *How much would it cost for a hotel?*
Vikram *Maybe about 600 or 700 . . . 700 for the bigger ones and 60 for the smaller ones.*

These pieces of dialogue clearly illustrate that the children have picked up a lot of incidental knowledge about the places that they have visited. This is all the more intriguing when one realises that these children were all less than six when they visited the countries that they chose to talk about. The accuracies in their knowledge, such as Bahts being the currency in Phuket, and the climate of the region are balanced out by the delightful, if inaccurate, reply to the question of what clothes were worn in Thailand – 'Ties of course'.

These children have all had experience of living in big hotels and for them the only alternative accommodation must be poor hotels. Time and time again in their play they discuss the merits of one hotel over another. They rarely talk about prices but the figures that they do come up with rarely bear any relationship to real costs. Expensive hotels are seen as costing sums which can be represented by high figures. They do, however, reflect an understanding of comparative numbers. You pay more for a bigger hotel or longer flight. They also demonstrate that they know people speak different languages in other countries. Thomas and Vicky had an interesting discussion which revealed that they understood the difference between a country and a continent. I really felt that these children had begun to grasp some basic geographical principles. They were concerned with what places are like, how locations affect peoples lives, and what people in different countries do. They even seem to have grasped the concept that people use and adapt their surroundings.

In the following extract William is taking the role of the travel agent and is talking about Malaysia.

> **Joey** *Me and Thomas would like to go for a holiday in Malaysia.*
> **William** *Which airline would you like to go on?*
> **Joey** *First we would like to go on the American airlines and then fly another distance to Malaysia. Can we get a direct flight to Hong Kong?*
> **William** *Yes.*
> **Thomas** *How many . . . what currents do you use in Malaysia?*
> **William** *You probably use dollars.*
> **Joey** *What type of typhoons are there?*
> **William** *There are not very windy typhoons.*
> **Thomas** *Are there any robbers?*
> **William** *Of course not!*
> **Thomas** *What are all the people like in Malaysia?*
> **William** *They're all brown . . . because of the sun . . . brown faces and some of them are white.*
> **Thomas** *Is there any good food in Malaysia?*
> **William** *Well, there's meat you put on a stick and eat it. It's very tasty.*
> **Thomas** *You mean Satay?*
> **William** *Yes.*
> **Thomas** *Are there any mountains in Malaysia?*

> **William** *Yes there's quite a lot of them.*
>
> **Joey** *Can you climb the mountains . . . are they climbing mountains?*
>
> **Thomas** *What do they do in Malaysia . . . what jobs?*
>
> **William** *Well there's one that they make tapes for the video and to sell them . . . some are making toys . . . some of them are going to work in a cemetary and some of them work in the airlines because a lot of people come to see the country.*

In this excerpt, William makes a completely non-racial reference to the colour of a Malay's skin. This is a feature of this type of play that I have observed over and over again – the complete acceptance of differences between cultures, beliefs and people. Another interesting cultural issue that was raised many times in dramatic role-play situations was that of different religions. The following conversation occurred when a group of children had been working with a December calendar, some travel brochures and timetables and were trying to work out the itinerary for a five-day Christmas break.

> **Daniel** *We're going to Phuket first and then Bankok.*
>
> **William** *What sort of churches is there?*
>
> **Joey** *There is Christian churches.*
>
> **Daniel** *Is there going to be Halloween . . . will there be snow for Halloween?*
>
> **Joey** *Yes but you won't be back there on time . . . it will be winter when you get back . . . some of the people there might be Buddhas . . . I mean Buddhists.*
>
> **William** *Is there any Hindus there?*
>
> **Daniel** *Will any be going to church on Sundays or not?*
>
> **Thomas** *Most on Saturdays.*
>
> **Daniel** *But what do you wear at Christmas?*
>
> **Lauren** *You should wear a coat and lots of warm things.*
>
> **Daniel** *But would you wear warm clothes if it was a hot country?*
>
> **Joey** *No.*
>
> **Daniel** *Is there always snow at Christmas.*
>
> **Lauren** *Well in some countries they do and some they don't . . . when they're near the South Pole they don't have any snow 'cos in Hong Kong they don't have snow but in England they have some but it's just really ice frost.*
>
> **Joey** *And in America too.*

Daniel *Because of the winds.*

Joey *It's because . . . yes the winds are blowing snow from the North Pole.*

Lauren *No . . . well the winds are blowing snow from the North Pole and because it's Jesus' birthday.*

Joey *The snow . . . makes . . . like a decoration for that!*

Daniel *Instead of having birthday parties for Jesus we don't have them . . . we have Christmas for Jesus' birthday and the wise men gave presents to Jesus at his birthday.*

The conversation then went on to discuss the role of Jesus versus Santa Claus in the Christmas story, but swings back to the holiday theme with the final question.

Vikram *How does Father Christmas know what hotels you've gone to?*

Daniel *You write or get a piece of plain paper or some pictures on it . . . then you write down the hotel and your address and whatever you want for Christmas and then you can send it to him.*

Joey *How can Father Christmas leave toys at a hotel.*

Vikram *He can leave them in a sack.*

Lauren *Or he can bring them in a sleigh.*

This dialogue, once again, illustrates beautifully the tolerance and openness which young children have to new ideas. This conversation developed into a discussion of comparative religion and then reverted to the intended theme in a completely natural way.

The travel agency has been in operation for most of the term and children from several classes used it. The children had written their own notices which are up on the wall inviting other children to write about their own countries or countries that they have visited. At the end of each week I check the pile of notices.

Thilini (aged six) had written:

Shri Lanka is hot and nice and has different words and money.

Erica (aged six) had written the following:

Erica
in Japan people live in Japanees castles. and disny land is in it Iv been to disny land three times in Japan. Japanees people Like raiss, sometimes they pray to god. they make Japanees food in Japanees restruns in Japanees there are little pink flouers on trees. Japanees people ware nice. dresses with butiful patens on them. Japanees people dance in the Japanee castles

Example 4 Erica's account of Japan

In Japan people live in Japanese castles and Disneyland is in it. I've been to Disneyland three times in Japan. Japanese people like rice, sometimes they pray to God. They make Japanese food in Japanese restaurants. In Japan there are pink flowers on trees. Japanese people wear nice dresses with beautiful patterns on them. Japanese people dance in the Japanese castles.

Daisy (aged six) who comes from Korea wrote the following:

Example 5 Daisy's account of Korea

The Korean people eat Korean food . . . beef . . . chicken and all kinds of Korean food. And some of the ladies in Korea wear long dresses and wear a bow on their heads.

Joyleen (aged six) who is an American Chinese wrote:

In Amirce they eat meet and fist food and they were T-shirt and shoate albays some times they were dessese and some of them can Spaek chenese and some time it Sowes this is Amirec Monny $1 $2 $3 $4 $5

Example 6 Joyleen's account of America

> *In America they eat meat and fast food and they wear T-shirts and shorts always. Sometimes they wear dresses and some of them can speak Chinese and sometimes it snows. This is American money: $1, $2, $3, $4, $5.*

Laura (aged 6) contributed:

> *I went to Kenya and there are a lot of wild animals. There are giraffes and elephants and antelopes. There was a hotel. It was beautiful. There was a water hole and you could see the animals come down and have a drink. We went on tours as well. I had my own camera so I could take pictures. Some people are black. Some have nice faces. There are more black faces than white.*

Another extension of this play project has been the involvement of several parents from different ethnic backgrounds, who have willingly given up time to sit in the travel agency and answer the children's questions. This has led to some interesting interaction where the children were, for the first time, looking to an adult for the correct answers. An example of this was when William asked whether you can have typhoons that are not windy, and was told that the word 'typhoon' actually means big wind in Chinese so that all typhoons must be windy. This was followed by a delightful, simple explanation of how a typhoon was formed. Every child in the group

I went to Kenya

there are a lot of
wild animals there
are graifes and
elephants and Antielops
there was a Hotel it
was baeuiful there
was a water hole
and you could see
the animas come
and have a drick
we went on tores
as well I had my
own camra so I
could take picthes
some pepde are black
some of them have
nice faces. there
more black fases
than white

Example 7 Laura's account of Kenya

discovered a new concept or built onto their own partially formed ideas. This type of parental involvement does not rely on well-travelled and highly articulate parents. The only necessary ingredient is a parent who is prepared to become involved and spend some time interacting with a group of children. The dramatic role-play also became very literate in the sense that the children saw some purpose in writing and used their developing skills to share their knowledge. They also used their numeracy skills when working out costs, timetables and juggling with calendars.

The final piece of dialogue that I am going to introduce takes place in the travel agency one Friday afternoon. Lauren has decided to be the travel agent and Vikram, Thomas, Daniel, and Joey are thinking of going to London. Thomas and Daniel may have visited London at some time in their lives but the others have never been there. It is also very interesting that Lauren was only three on the only visit she has ever made to London.

Vikram *What sort of money do they use?*

Lauren *They use pennies and sometimes notes.*

Joey *Do you go by British Airways?*

Lauren *Well you go by a plane called . . . um . . . European Airlines.*

Vikram *Are there lots of hotels?*

Lauren *Yes lots of them. I only know three of them. One is called the Galeous Hotel, one is called the Stardust Hotel, and one is called the New Harbour Hotel.*

Daniel *What famous places do you visit?*

Lauren *You can visit the Palace where the Queen is and you can visit a famous hotel called Luxury Homes and you can go to one of the Queen's best restaurants called the fish 'n chip shop.*

Joey *Is there any temples there?*

Lauren *Quite a few.*

Thomas *What kind of weather is there?*

Lauren *Most of all it is windy, rainy, and cloudy but sometimes it is sunny.*

Thomas *Is it in Europe?*

Lauren *Um . . . well it is in Europe . . . it is near Europe and Wales.*

Vikram *What customs do they have at Christmas?*

Lauren *Well, sometimes they have people going to doors singing and collecting . . . people I think . . . to sing carols and when they finish the last door they all sing looking up and putting their hands together and singing some Jesus songs and then go back home.*

Vikram *Would you like to live in England better than Hong Kong and why?*

Lauren *Well I do like to live in England much more because I love fish and chips.*

Daniel *Is there many koalas, cats, dogs and pigs?*

Lauren *Well there is dogs, cats, deers, koalas, pigs.*

Thomas *Do they get kangaroos?*

Lauren *Well, there is some in zoos.*

Vikram *Thomas and me would like to go for a holiday in London. Could you book it for us?*

Lauren *OK . . . but you're just in time because the British Airways and the Travel Europe is going . . . landing in three hours. Which would you like to fly on?*

Thomas *British Airways.*

Lauren *Well, the British Airways is the normal plane but the Europe Airways is Concorde and its expensive.*

Daniel *You are going to the National Hotel. Your room number is going to be 85 and your telephone number 865730.*

Vikram *How much does our bedroom cost?*

Lauren *Six dollars, but I will tell you in pounds as well . . . well you can have it for five pounds a bed . . . you can stay in a hotel and have bed and breakfast and eat your meal for three days.*

Vikram *Where can we visit?*

Lauren *You can go to places where there is lots of restaurants . . . you can go to places like British Home Stores shopping centre and all sorts of stuff.*

Joey *Is that all?*

Lauren *Don't forget to bring your warm clothes and I will try to arrange for you to go to Buckingham Palace.*

Thomas *That will be good.*

Vikram *Will we actually meet the Queen?*

Lauren *Well . . . you could . . . but sometimes the guards won't let you in. Here . . . have this ticket . . . if you show it to the guards they might let you in because my Granny knows the Queen very well.*

Vikram *Could we see Prince Charles and Princess Diana?*

Lauren *Well . . . Princess Diana is normally with the Queen and Prince Charles is normally in Wales.*

Conclusion

This piece of role-play shows quite clearly that even young children can use their play situations to gain insights and knowledge about their environment and the world they live in. They acquire this experience from first-hand experience, from listening, from books, from the media and from each other. Through play they are able to test out this knowledge in a safe environment where there is no right or wrong answer, as every viewpoint is valid. The children in my school have had many opportunities to travel around the world and visit new places. I believe, however, that the experiences of all children could be drawn on in a similar way to develop their geographical concepts. Even if children have never left their home town, a tourist office could be established in the classroom. The children could plan expeditions and visits for tourists in their area, and look at public transport routes and places to stay in the neighbourhood. Parents could be involved as consultants, and brochures and posters could be produced. The resulting play would be truly cross-curricular and a valuable extension to the primary curriculum.

8 The airport as one world
Laura Sparrow

Most primary teachers would accept that there is an important need to provide children with real and relevant experiences in school which will enable them to make some sense of themselves, their families, culture and community. Additionally, there is the need for them to be acquainted with notions of ethnicity, cultural diversity, and the equivalence of both individuals and groups if they are to participate without prejudice in a modern multifaceted world.

A school's multicultural policy should commit it to specific action to prioritise areas such as environment, curriculum, management, discipline, employment and handling strategies, attitudes and sensitivities, for the promotion of equal opportunities and the process of countering racism. Practical steps towards achieving this should be outlined clearly for everyone. Implementing such a policy is never very easy, and for primary schools it will be particularly problematic unless a good deal of thought is applied.

One possibility is to seek to achieve such ends through structured play. To ensure that such ends are realised the development of a play setting needs particular attention. Any old situation will not do. The play situation has to be able to encompass a number of critical features. It must aim to be relatively realistic both in its surface features and in providing the underlying relationships inherent in a real-life version; it must represent the real world. It must be fairly complex. Real life is complex as are most problems which involve human relationships. The development of children's sensitivity towards other people is unlikely to be achieved in situations which cut out or reduce opportunities for facing and resolving confrontation and differences in opinion. The situation must be one in which children care about the consequences of their actions and decisions because they have implications which affect other people's lives. The situation must represent a world where a large number of people need to work together, and where working together has to be 'worked at'; in other words the play situation must be like a small world in which many human behaviours, feelings, attitudes and beliefs are integrated within an overall structure.

With these considerations in mind, we attempted to establish a context for creating such a world. We set up an airport for four middle- and top-infant classes in a large, empty practical area which was being used for groups to work on art activities with our nursery nurse. The building was modern and had the advantage of low ceilings and two sinks, one of which was later used in the airplane galley. As the project involved four classes, about four weekly meetings were necessary to plan the project, decide its components, map and plan the area, and to collect resources. These took place about one month before we started. Once the project was underway, weekly meetings were important to us as we had to plan the weekly programme of activities with the nursery nurse. We also needed to share, review and discuss the children's responses and progress. As many of the children in the school were bilingual, we also had the advantage of being able to involve Section eleven staff in the work in the area, and to ensure that they became an important part of the airport team.

The airport is an excellent example of a realistic situation and one which, in its basic organisation, demanded cooperation, coordination and interdependence. More significantly, it afforded a means to reach a recognition of the importance of all the various participants. The airport presented a notion of a broad, organic, multifaceted whole which only succeeds when everybody does his or her share. It provided practical first-hand experience with which children could readily identify. In essence, the airport provided a learning frame into which the children could incorporate their previous existing knowledge and upon which they could develop their conceptual understanding.

With its many interlinking parts, it soon became clear to the children that it was only when all the components were successfully cooperating together that the airport worked. This became an ideal paradigm of a society or 'one world'. It enabled the setting up of problems, searches for solutions, posing of questions, and the transfer of skills into the real world, outside school. Conflict, and its resolution, became a primary motivating feature for discussion, and ultimately it allowed for a real understanding that if one constituent part fails, serious ramifications may result for the whole organisation. For example, if there were to be a pay strike by the baggage handlers, the flight would have to be delayed or even cancelled because the passengers couldn't leave without their luggage.

Planning the airport as a model of one world

We felt strongly that the airport needed to be very big and factually correct if it were going to succeed, and we modelled it on Manchester Airport, to which we made many visits with the children as we were setting it up. We were able to arrange with British Airways for the children to actually sit down on a 727 shuttle to London during a visit. Our airport consisted of: a waiting room, travel agency, ticket counter, canteen, control tower, engine workshop, airport gift shop, newspaper stand, passport control, security x-ray machine, baggage trolleys, petrol pump, crew and staff. In the aeroplane we had a cabin, galley, cockpit, and crew.

We started the project by establishing our aims. These included:

1 To develop the idea of one world in which people are interrelated and interdependent.
2 To look at the organisation of the airport, stressing it as a complex whole requiring cooperative skills and an ability to deal with problems. To examine cooperation of people and interlinking of services which makes the airport successful.
3 To look at people's conflicting needs: disabled, elderly, young, etc. and to examine clear conflicts: people wanting the same things, planes requiring servicing simultaneously, organising rotas, disputes.
4 To examine cultural and language similarities in the airport, use of translation, time change, climate, other features of common experience.

For achieving these aims we developed objectives, drew out a layout, and finally devised a skills chart which addressed concepts, skills and activities which we were interested in teaching. For instance, our chart for 'Social skills' included:

1 Negotiating the roles of people working at the airport, and the roles of people and families using the airport.
2 Negotiating the shared use of space by groups working in the airport area.
3 Negotiating within contrived situations, clear conflicts.
4 Mastering conversation appropriate to specific contexts in the airport.

Such skills were worked out across a whole range of areas. A clear spiral was then set which commenced with aims, focused on skills, implemented by activities, requiring specific resources which we needed to achieve our aims. It will be clear that a great deal more was involved than just providing a set of props and leaving the children to get on with it. For the staff this is a demanding, intellectual activity, but it has the virtue of allowing us to understand fully what it is we are doing when we make claims about the learning potential of play in the curriculum.

Setting up the airport: the component features

1 The travel agency
This consisted of a table with globes, maps, charts, air routes, timetables, brochures, posters, and travel information collected from the airport and travel agents. A scrapbook of all relevant work done by the children was kept here. An environment saturated with print: captions, labels, word banks, adverts, and posters was provided. Role-plays, with children as well as teachers asking for information were very popular. The headteacher was sometimes spotted enquiring about holidays to Pakistan or the Caribbean (when he should have been elsewhere!).

2 Ticket counter
Sales people made out tickets, provided travellers with forms to fill in prior to their flights, and collected and dispensed information about departures and destinations, take-off and arrival times, and any dietary requirements for passengers (such as vegetarian, hellal, salt-free diets). Tickets were

priced, money was exchanged, and complaints were noted. A visiting lecturer from Manchester Polytechnic was sold a ticket to Bombay but was reported to have arrived too late for the flight.

3 Passport control

Children designed their own passports and put in all relevant information on various forms before making the final version. Distinguishing features were recorded by children about themselves: age, height, weight, date of birth, place of birth, etc. They loved designing stamps and stamping their passports. Various self-esteem activities came to the fore here as children wrote on their forms such things as 'I can speak three languages fluently and am very good at doing sums 1–20.'

4 Control tower

The control tower was in constant communication with incoming and outbound planes. On a table, we had a large control panel with many switches, knobs and lights corresponding to runways and air lanes. At first the 'radio' was imaginary, and a child ran as a messenger between the tower and the cockpit. Later, we got some walkie-talkies, which had an astonishing effect in uplifting the quality of conversation. This proved fascinating, particularly as the tower officers sometimes got involved in intense negotation between different pilots arguing to land or take off. Holding patterns, fires, emergencies, hijacks, crashes and procedures were established by the children. The quality of this dialogue was extremely impressive.

5 Airport gift shop and international news stand

This had a distinctly international feel, with a display of world newspapers and a rich variety of toys, gifts and clothes. There were some objects sold which many of the teachers were envious of, but which the shop had to retain for its own stock. In this way, artefacts, clothes, and unusual items from different cultures could be investigated and played with in a natural, neutral manner.

6 Baggage handlers/freight parcels/clothes trolley

We had many different sizes and styles of baggage with a wide range of clothing for all types of people and all kinds of climates. A large wall display showing clothes for hot countries and clothes for cold countries in a large set ring informed children about appropriateness of materials and styles for dress, and photos of people in different parts of the world visually established why some cultures may adopt certain forms of attire. One teacher set up a rock star's suitcase with a lot of different clues as to who it might be and where that person might be going, and she changed it weekly. Children were found arguing over the contents during dinner time, when they should have been outside. A good selection of parcels of different sizes, shapes and weights were available for fitting on to trolleys, estimating, weighing, and pricing. Luggage was transported by handlers, along with freight, on to the plane. Passengers were encouraged to pack their bags from a wide selection of dressing up items depending on the sort of holiday they had chosen, (ice-skating, skiing, beach, requiring ice-skates, gloves, or shorts and sunglasses etc.)

7 Fuel tanker and taxi stand
An old book trolley was fitted with large plastic tubing for fuelling the airplane. This was a very important component, as was the taxi stand and the other airport vehicles, as it provided an opportunity for shy children or children whose English was limited to participate in a low-profile sort of way in an important role. Other children were able to integrate them into the play activity and make them feel included in what was going on elsewhere. These vehicles were normally made of large cupboard boxes, with a crate for the steering wheel.

8 Airport waiting room
The walls of the waiting room were occupied by life-size collages of busy people flying in and out from all over the world. People from many different ethnic origins were selected, and were made by the children drawing around each other and designing their style of dress. There was considerable discussion involved in their choosing, producing and displaying these people and the children became aware of the need for balance and fairness in selecting where people should go on the wall. A drinks machine was also made for the waiting room. It was designed by the children, constructed of a long cardboard box, and proved very popular with our travellers.

9 The airplane: galley/cabin/cockpit
The airplane was constructed by setting out rows of chairs with an aisle in between and a suspended corrugated card side with round window holes cut out to suggest the look of a plane. The cockpit was made from an old toy house frame which was painted and heavily decorated with dials, buttons, meters, levers and switches. The galley was set up at the back of the cabin and was equipped with trays, trolleys, and food made by the children from

painted dough. A lot of set work based on menus was done in the galley, linked to the ticket counter forms for special diets.

Ongoing activities

Each constituent area was stocked with ongoing activities from which children could freely choose to work. A large practical activity table was laid out in the middle of the airport with creative materials necessary for the production of items required for the airport such as the collages of travellers for the waiting room, parachutes, dough, passports, gliders, etc. and was varied daily. Each area was well resourced with workcards, information sheets, and worksheets requiring children to conduct interviews, questionnaires, surveys, graphs and charts, and the collection of information about children's flying experience, holiday patterns and family origins.

A strong science focus required children to design and produce different sorts of paper gliders and parachutes, testing materials for lightness, propulsion and speed properties, and wind resistance. Samples of work were collected and displayed on walls, and suspended from ceilings. Photo displays about airplanes, places around the world and people were put up. A large six foot paper-mâché model of Concorde was designed and constructed by the children and hung up. Maps of the airport were drawn and a three-dimensional model of it with runways, buildings and planes was set out on a table and became a focal point for play with small model planes and vehicles. Children worked in pairs, in groups, as individuals, and occassionally, in class units. A flexible form of organisation and usage was encouraged.

One world: role-play and conflict

It was surprisingly easy to establish equivalent but conflicting needs in the airport. In the ticket office, arguments about who should be given the last seat on the airplane were rapidly taken on board by children when an elderly person in a wheelchair was brought forward at the same time as a woman with a young baby. Whose need was more pressing? How should a selection be made? What criteria could be identified for making such decisions in the future? Disputes over working routines were hotly contested in the control tower when the fuel tanker operators complained that their equipment had broken down, while the pilots were anxiously waiting for take-off clearance. Baggage handlers might be slow with their loading of cargo, causing worry and panic for the cabin crew as passengers complained about the delay.

Varied conflicts requiring immediate resolution permeated all features of the airport's functioning. In the control tower, two planes were requesting clearance for take-off at the same time. Planes would be stacked up for landing requiring designated runways. Wheelchairs and prams were requested by different cabin staff, and shortages and breaking down of equipment caused pressure. People required standby tickets on flights which were overbooked. Strikes were not uncommon, and shifts needed rotas and named personnel sorting out by children.

All of these situations posed problems demanding discussion, asking questions, providing arguments, analysis and brainstorming for their solution. Priorities had to be defined, decisions made with identifiable criteria which were determined by children. These quite sophisticated conflicts were introduced slowly and re-introduced in graduated complexity. The children proved themselves to be most adept at diplomatic solutions and ideas, enabling and empowering them to feel directive, involved and determined in using their developing skills. Their performance was astonishing. The more their ideas and observations were incorporated into the provision, activities and resourcing, the broader their application of skills and concepts became.

The frequent posing of hiccups in practical organisation helped to stress to children the crucial importance of cooperation in the real world. The interdependence between the ground-based crews and the air-based crews was clearly appreciated by all the children. Gradually, they came to see the importance of all the contributors, both high and low profile, and a perception of the necessity of people working together was identified as the highest priority. From this concrete example of linkage and interdependence, we were able to establish a more abstract concept of respect for all participating individuals. Finally there could be a clear view of the airport as the world, and of our world as one world.

One world: the airport as a collaborative experience

The airport was visited by many children and adults. The overriding observations reported to staff were concerned with the high levels of confidence which the children working in the airport demonstrated. In particular, the seriousness with which the children undertook their roles and instructed one another, and the concentration and effort which they put into tasks were thought by observers to be quite remarkable. The children themselves were self-critical of their own performances and indicated increasingly heightened expectations of themselves ('I could have done that better.'). But there was always another opportunity to do so as the airport was there for a term.

Some video-taping of children playing in the airport was carried out and shown to the children, who commented on their roles, often with honesty and great perception, once they got over the initial shock of seeing themselves on television. Discussions with groups of children studying the video were focused on analysis of how well the groups worked together and how their cooperative process might be improved. More than anything else, a sense of great pride and excellence in themselves, and an appreciation of the quality of caring in their small community emerged from this. An attitudinal learning spiral was set up, with the children's commitment to the situation being enhanced by their growing self-confidence and sense of achievement through learning more each day.

Finally, most significantly, the children's sensitivity to themselves and to others was also appreciably affected, particularly with respect to their tolerance of individual needs. This was noticeable with their perceptions of race and disabilty. As in any school, there were some tensions regarding a few children who were new, and who were experiencing some problems settling in. These children happened to have an obvious physical disability, or an ethnic dissimilarity. We were able to use the issues extraced from the conflict resolution work in the airport to make linkages with the needs of these particular children. As we had already presented the role-plays involving disabled people, we were able to develop through later discussion, a response which was based on a true understanding of what our disabled youngsters negotiated every day in school. In this way, a real appreciation of the nature of disadvantage was presented to children in a manner which was realistic and relevant, but at the same time, neutral and safe. Additionally, the brilliance and bravery of those children could be clearly perceived, supported and praised by others. This leap in conceptual reciprocity was tremendous and marvellous to witness and made the airport one-world experience inspirational to all of us who were involved.

[This chapter is written in dedication to Misba Haq, who died aged twelve, on 18.10.90. Her life was a shining example of courage and spirit to everyone who knew her.]

9 Getting from the railway station to the hotel

Helen Strahan

I recently spent some time working with a group of teachers exploring the use of structured play in schooling. The intention was to set up a play area that would be shared by all the younger children (the nursery and infant children) and subsequently to extend the use of play into the junior department of the school.

Although I had been a teacher at the school I was at the time seconded to Manchester Polytechnic. As part of that secondment I was working back at my school in this collaborative enquiry in to play. With the teachers and younger children we had established a structured play area around the theme of a railway station. This had been extremely successful. Visits to stations had been made, and the development of the area had been discussed with many of the children. Most of the children had contributed in some way to the establishment of the area and all were, at various times, allowed to use it. The area, which was available for use by all the children, comprised a train, booking office, and many of the shops and kiosks that would normally be found at a station. The use of the station area was extremely dynamic at all age levels as some of my observations will show.

Observation 1 – Reception class (4/5 years)

> (Talk re destinations) 'Can we all use the same train?' Some said yes and
> some no – this became quite heated and noisy. Then the driver said 'Well
> it doesn't matter if we've gone passed Liverpool, we'll go backwards and

then we'll go to . . . (another child shouted 'London') . . . London and Blackpool. Everyone seemed happy with this.

Observation 2 – Year One (5/6 years)

> **Jamie** *Check the engines, the steam is stuck, lift up the seat! (Slight tussle with Simon who was sitting on the seat.)*
>
> **Simon** *OK then can I mend it now?*
>
> **Jamie** *No! – Oh all right, you can help.*
>
> **Simon** *Pretend you've fixed it now – let's sit here (both sit down on seat).*

Observation 3 – Year Two (6/7 years)

> **Amy** *. . . no you can't just go – you're the driver – it's not a station yet, you can't go to the toilet while you're driving.*
>
> **Paul** *Well there's toilets on trains!*
>
> **Ami** *Yes but not for the driver or there'd be a crash.*
>
> **Paul** *Station! We're at the station. Get out for Blackpool. Right I'm going to the toilet – we'll be leaving for Manchester in a bit – mind the train.*

In addition to the dynamic nature of the talk, considerable use was made of writing. Another of my observations indicates some of this usage.

> *Child (aged six) standing in ticket collector's kiosk using paper and pen found at the post office to conduct a survey of how many times she clipped people's tickets. She began by writing people's names down every time they came through, but then decided by herself that it would be easier just to put a tick beside the name after the first occasion (see Example 1).*

Example 1 Conducting a survey

Successful though this experience was for the children, only part of the intention had been achieved. The second, and principal, aim was to see if play could be incorporated in the school lives of older children. Part of the problem was convincing teachers of older children that such an aim was feasible. As one teacher put it:

> *I think play is really important and juniors should have the chance, but there are more things in the way here – it's not what we do – children don't have things to play with and work comes first.*

These were the words of a junior teacher being explicit about her recognition that although play is important in theory, there are barriers when it comes to putting theory into practice, especially where older children are concerned. It's not enough just to think that it is important. This teacher was speaking at a joint infant/junior staff meeting when we were trying to decide how to introduce a structured play area into the junior department.

There were two issues that were important to us. The first was that there should be continuity of experience across the infant and the junior department. The second was that the junior children should 'own' the activity in the same way as the infant children had.

The first issue, apart from its general relevance in primary education, held particular importance and problems for us; we were working in a newly amalgamated primary school still on a split site. Thus there were already problems of separation between the two departments. The second arose from our recognition that the undoubted success of the infant railway station had much to do with the amount of autonomy the children had been allowed in setting it up. We also realised that it was not just teachers who had feelings that 'playing' was not the way learning was done at school: the junior children also had fairly definite ideas that whilst play was a good thing outside the school context, in school it was either 'naughty' or 'babyish'. It was important for us as teachers that we not only challenged our own assumptions but challenged those of the children as well.

An obvious starting point seemed to be to involve the junior staff and children in the infant area. We focused on the obvious link between Year Two and Year Three but we also explored the perceptions of Year Six – they were the children furthest from the infants in age but the most influential (and hopefully the most perceptive) group of children in the junior department. The Year Two and Year Three teachers organised some joint sessions in the infant's railway station. The older children came across to the infant building and played with the infant children, as well as on their own in the station.

This 'playing' gave teachers the opportunity to step back and look at what the groups from their respective classes were actually doing when they were playing. The infants had introduced rules into even the free play sessions in the railway station (at other times teachers would ask children to assume certain roles or assign them specific tasks), and they explained these to the juniors. Both teachers were impressed that given the differences in academic and social ability between and across classes, there was little conflict and a lot of cooperation. This experience challenged the usual behaviours at transition from infant to junior; instead of the infants going to the junior building in the role of learners, they were taking on the role of teachers while, at the same time, allowing their future teacher to see them in an environment where they felt comfortable and in control.

There is not space in this chapter for me to explore all the interactions and events that took place as part of this exploration and I intend to concentrate here upon how the Year Six involvement developed from using the infants' railway station to setting up their own structured play area in the junior department.

The older children's explorations of play

The first time that the Year Six children played in the railway station they assigned themselves roles very quickly and stuck with them for significant periods of time – between twenty-five minutes and an hour. They did not seem to need the reassurance of teachers either joining in with or leading the play and quickly became absorbed and apparently unconscious of the video camera that was being used to record what happened. Indeed, when I intervened after half-an-hour and suggested to the four children who had taken over the running of the ticket office that they were a little out of the main action and might like to change, they told me that they were 'just getting in to it' and wanted to carry on working out a more efficient booking system.

On the main station there were very few changes – these children seemed to appreciate the opportunity to really get into the role from the word go. A boy and a girl (who did not normally play together) had taken over joint charge of the station. They spoke in a very official manner using 'posh' voices and wrote notes about things that they felt were needed, for example a megaphone, and in this particular case they also sketched how to make one if they couldn't borrow the real thing. The juniors did not seem to want to try everything at once as the infants had generally done when first using the station. On subsequent occasions these children decided that they should change because 'It wouldn't be fair otherwise'.

The Year Six children all had the opportunity to play in the railway station, both on their own and with the younger children. They were then asked by their class teacher, who had not been with them, to think critically about what the infant children were learning. This is what one child wrote:

"The infants have a structured play area. What is structured play? Structured play is where people learn and play. Their structured play area is about railways. We saw there skills such as.

Communication

They were communicating with other people on telephones. They talked and listened to each other on the phone as if there was some one really there.

Social

The children were working together, Sharing their toy money and beining patient in the queue in the ticket shop. They met each other on the train and made friends. The signs told them where to go.

Math's

The ticket girls asked for the money lik- 69 p please and the infants found out by counting it and learning how much it was. They learnt the time by watching and listening to it. Also they learnd the time by watching the time tables. They constructed their models so they would work. This means they are learning how to plan together"

Example 2 A ten-year-old's view on learning from play

The infants have a structured play area. What is structured play?
Structured play is where people learn and play. Their structured play
area is about railways. We saw their skills such as:

Communication

They were communicating with other people on telephones. They talked
and listened to each other on the phone as if there was someone really
there.

Social

The children were working together, sharing their toy money and being
patient in the queue in the ticket shop. They met each other on the train
and made friends. The signs told them where to go.

Maths

The ticket girls asked for the money like – '69p please' – and the infants
found out by counting it and learning how much it was. They learned the
time by watching and listening to it. Also they learned the time by
watching the time tables. They constructed their models so they would
work. This means they are learning how to plan together.

This piece of writing has been included in its entirety because readers may
find the categories that the child has used interesting. Other children tended
to be more general in their approach, but some of them were very perceptive
(at no point had the children been told what to write or given categories for
observing the younger children's behaviour). The older children identified
things like:

> When I was playing with a girl called Lisa she was sharing her ticket with
> me. I also noticed that they were learning to do things in order, like go to
> the ticket box, go and get it clipped, get into the train and so on.

> They learnt how to use the phone by dialling the numbers and finding
> which numbers they had to use in the book.

> When they were building the train station they were learning how to
> construct and count things . . .

They were learning how to read timetables, how to tell the time and how to communicate by using the telephone. They were also learning how to write messages and read numbers and write them.

The infants constructed the station there self so they know where everything goes.

By this stage both Year Three and Year Six children were asking for a structured play area in the junior building. We discussed the best way of going about this with the older children. The main points that emerged from the discussion were:

1   The infant children had decided how the railway station should look, be resourced and be used. Teachers had helped and had given support and guidance, but had been willing to be overruled.
2   The junior children should decide on the theme for the structured play area.
3   To do this they all needed knowledge of what was involved.
4   There should be an election to decide on a theme so that every child in the juniors could have a say.

After further debate these ideas became the basis for the following plan of action:

1   The older children would do an assembly about structured play and their experiences in the railway station. They would use the videos we had made of both infants and juniors playing there.
2   After the assembly each class was to elect two representatives to come to a meeting with the older children. Two teachers would also come along (the teachers were there to give guidance when necessary but were not allowed to 'take over').
3   Each class was to come up with a list of ideas for a possible structured play area. These ideas would be drawn up into a final list at a second class representative's meeting.
4   Voting on the list would take place in each class.

The headteacher and junior staff all agreed to this action plan and it went ahead. A hotel was decided upon by a large majority. There then followed the same sort of visit and negotiation period as had occurred prior to the setting up of the railway station. However, nothing ever goes quite to plan in a school; the school was being repainted while all this was going on and the area designated for the structured play area was constantly being used as an overflow classroom and paint and scaffolding store! A reception area was quickly set up in the downstairs corridor, which doubled as a general school reception area for parents and other visitors.

Obviously we looked at many issues during the project such as planning, monitoring, assessment, parent and staff involvement and participation, cross-curricularity and, of course, infant/junior continuity. We also spent a lot of time exploring practical ways of integrating structured play into ordinary classroom practice (we might not always have the space and we certainly would not normally have the luxury of a member of staff on secondment with so much time to coordinate matters).

The Year Six action stemmed from a realisation that the infant children had a large measure of freedom in setting up their structured play area and that they enjoyed using it because they owned it. There was a definite sense that the juniors understood the importance of continuing in this way, as the following extract from a discussion that I had with a group of Junior 4 children shows:

> **Alex** . . . *those children made it themselves so they really know it, they can do what they like there.*
> **Me** *Do you really think so? I can think of a few things that they wouldn't be allowed to do there.*
> **Sonia** *Yes but they wouldn't want to do anything really bad.*
> **Tim** *Some of them might!*
> **Sonia** *No because it's dead good and then it . . . they wouldn't be allowed.*
> **Carol** *You don't like smash or anything your own stuff do you?*
> **Peter** *When we've done the hotel that will be something for all the juniors that will be theirs – like in the infants.*

The older children had recognised a number of important qualities necessary to the setting up and implementation of their structured play area. They identified the importance of 'being able to get on with each other – cooperating and helping', 'not being bossy', 'needing to talk a lot – so that everybody knows how each other feels', 'listening to each other', 'being sensible – thinking before speaking and doing something', 'being well organised'.

The one thing that was noticeably different with the junior play was the level and type of teacher intervention. Obviously the role of the teacher was something that we constantly debated. We were concerned about the balance between being over-directive and stifling the children's spontaneity and making sure that play did not become repetitive and boring. Generally speaking this was more of a worry at infant level; as the children got older they seemed more able to sustain play which was self-initiated and involved complex problem solving and idea generation.

It was interesting that the juniors, and the Year Six class in particular, seemed to be less affected by sex role stereotyping. Very few of them appeared to think that station masters or hotel managers 'should' be male or that receptionists 'should' be female. Some of the younger children had found it difficult to abandon these ideas. They also expressed more positive interest in the various newspapers and magazines available that were written in scripts they could not understand (the school was totally monolingual and almost monocultural) – perhaps a small indication that our commitment to equal opportunities and anti-racism was having some sort of cumulative effect.

The influence of popular culture was more obvious in the 'hotel' play created by the Year Six children. We had a lot of scenes adapted from *Dallas* and *Dynasty* – possibly influenced by a visit to a very expensive hotel in the city centre where, when we were told how much it cost to stay the night, two children spontaneously commented, 'That's more than my mum gets in a week' and 'I bet that's a lot more than you earn isn't it Miss?'

The reception area of the hotel seemed to bridge the gap between work and play very well for those children (particularly the younger juniors) who were initially uncertain about playing in school. They could sit in the corridor and be very involved in the life of the school outside their immediate classroom – greeting visitors, taking telephone messages and at the same time being involved in similar activities to do with the hotel. This is reflected in a small piece of conversation I had with two Year Five children sitting at the reception desk.

> **Me** *So this is what you are working on when the area is quiet?*
> **Kahil** *Yes, or when we want to do something else.*
> **Me** *How far have you got?*

Sam *We know the area of this bedroom now and we've got a diagram that's scale. So we're just seeing if we really can fit another bed, another single in. I don't think its OK really.*

Kahil *He thinks there won't be enough space but I think we can move the table. I think we'll have to do some furniture for the . . . to stick on.*

The way in which we managed the project impressed upon junior children the importance of their earlier experience with the younger children and gave them some sense of the oneness of the school. It also gave the older children a clear idea of themselves as leaders in innovation, whilst not allowing them to forget that younger children and staff were also important to the success of the project . . .

Me *. . . so just tell me again about your plans for getting the other teachers involved.*

William *They know things already from you and Mrs Scott and their classes will have told them.*

Holly *Yes and the assembly . . . when they have all watched the video and everyone thinks its dead good and all, they'll help the kids – well I think so.*

Simon *Everyone knows – like all Mrs Hunt's class (Junior 1) and all the infants on the video – they will be like they're in assembly telling them.*

Me *Telling them what?*

William *Showing the teachers what they can do, but we can do it better . . . we're older and we've been in the infants already.*

Simon *Yes we know how to do more things and the teachers can help us.*

Helen *Hey! Perhaps the infant teachers can tell the junior teachers how to do things – you have meetings don't you!*

Me *Yes – although I don't think 'tell' is a very good word, you were the one who was talking earlier about people having freedom to accept or reject what you said!*

Helen *Discuss then!*

Conclusion

Generally we felt that we had been reasonably successful as far as infant/junior continuity and children's ownership of learning went. Some things were still 'in the way', but we had made a start in both thinking about and creating actual play in the juniors. Both staff and children felt they had learnt a lot. Indeed, the way the staff felt they were learning was one of the most powerful features of the project. This is shown clearly in the following extract from an interview conducted with her teacher by a ten-year-old.

> **Child** *What do you think you would be learning if you were doing structured play?*
>
> **Teacher** *I am doing structured play.*
>
> **Child** *No – if you were in it.*
>
> **Teacher** *I am in it and I am learning things, because I've not really done structured play before so I'm learning from it as well. I'm learning alongside you really, things that you're learning . . . how to set things up and how you can bring it into school and make people realise its not play as in when we go outside and have a run round – that it's worthwhile and leads onto other things here in school and that all areas of our school day can be brought into structured play.*

A project in which both children and teachers recognise that they are learning is an extremely powerful one for a school.

R